A New Voyage [
World, in the years
and 26, Vo

Otto von Kotzebue

Alpha Editions

This edition published in 2022

ISBN: 9789356785052

Design and Setting By

Alpha Editions

www.alphaedis.com

Email - info@alphaedis.com

Contents

KAMTSCHATKA

THE wind, which continued favourable to us as far as the Northern Tropic, was succeeded by a calm that lasted twelve days. The ocean, as far as the eye could reach, was as smooth as a mirror, and the heat almost insupportable. Sailors only can fully understand the disagreeableness of this situation. The activity usual on shipboard gave place to the most wearisome idleness. Every one was impatient; some of the men felt assured that we should never have a wind again, and wished for the most violent storm as a change.

One morning we had the amusement of watching two great sword-fish sunning themselves on the surface of the water. I sent out a boat, in the hope that the powerful creatures would, in complaisance, allow us the sport of harpooning them, but they would not wait; they plunged again into the depths of the sea, and we had disturbed their enjoyments in vain.

Our water-machine was several times let down, even to the depth of a thousand fathoms: on the surface, the temperature was 24°, and at this depth, only 2° of Reaumur.

On the 22nd of May, the anniversary of our frigate's leaving Stopel, we got a fresh easterly wind, which carried us forward pretty quickly on the still smooth surface of the sea.

On the 1st of June, when in latitude 42° and longitude 201°, and consequently opposite the coast of Japan, we descried a red stripe in the water, about a mile long and a fathom broad. In passing over it we drew up a pail-full, and found that its colour was occasioned by an infinite number of crabs, so small as to be scarcely distinguishable by the naked eye.

We now began daily to experience increasing inconveniences from the Northern climate. The sky, hitherto so serene, became gloomy and covered with storm-clouds, which seldom threatened in vain; we were, besides, enveloped in almost perpetual mists, bounding our prospect to a few fathoms. In a short time, the temperature of the air had fallen from 24° to 3°. So sudden a change is always disagreeable, and often dangerous. We had to thank the skill and attention of our physician, Dr. Siegwald, that it did not prove so to us. Such rough weather is not common to the latitude we were in at that season; but it is peculiar to the Japanese coast even in summer. Whales and storm-birds showed themselves in great numbers, reminding us that we were hastening to the North, and were already far from the luxuriant groves of the South-Sea islands.

The wind continued so favourable, that on the 7th of June we could already see the high mountains of Kamtschatka in their winter clothing. Their jagged summits reaching to the heavens, crested with everlasting snow, which glitters in the sunbeams, while their declivities are begirt with clouds, give a magnificent aspect to this coast. On the following day, we reached Awatscha Bay, and in the evening anchored in the harbour of St. Peter and St. Paul.

The great peninsula of Kamtschatka, stretching to the river Anadir on the North, and South to the Kurilian Islands, bathed on the east by the ocean, and on the west by the sea of Ochotsk, is, like many men, better than its reputation. It is supposed to be the roughest and most desolate corner of the world, and yet it lies under the same latitude as England and Scotland, and is equal in size to both. The summer is indeed much shorter, but it is also much finer; and the vegetation is more luxuriant than in Great Britain. The winter lasts long, and its discomforts are increased by the quantity of snow that falls; but in the southern parts the cold is moderate; and experience has repeatedly refuted the erroneous opinion, that on account of its long duration, and the consequent curtailment of the summer season, corn cannot be efficaciously cultivated here.

Although the snow lies in some of the valleys till the end of May, because the high, over-shadowing mountains intercept the warm sunbeams, yet garden-plants prosper. Potatoes generally yield a triple crop, and would perfectly supply the want of bread, if the inhabitants cultivated them more diligently: but the easier mode of providing fish in super-abundance as winter food, has induced them to neglect the labour of raising potatoes, although they have known years when the fishery has barely protected them from famine.

The winter, as I have already said, is very unpleasant, from the heavy snows, which, drifting from the mountains, often bury the houses, so that the inhabitants are compelled to dig a passage out, while the cattle walk on its frozen surface over their roofs.

Travelling in this season is very rapid and convenient. The usual mode is in sledges drawn by six or more dogs. The only danger is from snow-storms. The traveller, surprised by this sudden visitation, has no chance for safety except in quietly allowing himself and his dogs to be buried in the snow, and relieving himself from his covering when the storm is past. This, however, is not always practicable; should the storm, or, as it is called here, "purga," overtake him in the ravine of a mountain, such an immense quantity of snow becomes heaped upon him, that he has no power to extricate himself from his tomb. These accidents, however, seldom occur; for the Kamtschatkans have acquired of necessity great foresight in meteorology, and of course never undertake a journey when they do not consider themselves sure of the weather.

The principal reason why the climate of Kamtschatka is inferior to that of other places under the same latitude, is to be found in the configuration of the country. The mountains of England, for instance, are of a very moderate height, and broken by extensive plains; here, on the contrary, intersected only by a few valleys of small extent, a single chain of mountains, its broken snow-crowned summits reaching to the clouds, and in many parts far beyond them, stretches the whole length of the Peninsula, and is based upon its breadth.

The panorama of Kamtschatka is a confused heap of granite blocks of various heights, thickly piled together, whose pointed, jagged forms bear testimony to the tremendous war of elements amidst which they must have burst from the bowels of the earth. The struggle is even now scarcely ended, as the smoking and burning of volcanoes, and frequent shocks of earthquake, sufficiently intimate. One of the mountains, called Kamtschatka Mountain, rivalling in height the loftiest in the world, often vomits forth streams of lava on the surrounding country. These mountains with their glaciers, and volcanoes emitting columns of fire and smoke from amidst fields of ice, afford a picturesque contrast with the beautiful green of the valleys. The most singular and indescribably-splendid effect is produced by the crystal rocks on the western coast, when illuminated by the sun; their whole refulgent surface reflecting his rays in every various tint of the most brilliant colours, resembles the diamond mountains of fairy-land, while the neighbouring rocks of quartz shine like masses of solid gold.

Kamtschatka is a most interesting country to the professor of the natural sciences. Great mineral treasures will certainly be one day discovered here; the number and diversity of its stones is striking even to the most uninitiated. It abounds in hot and salutary springs. To the botanist it offers great varieties of plants, little if at all known; and the zoologist would find here, amongst the animal tribes deserving his attention, besides several kinds of bears, wolves and foxes, the celebrated sable whose skin is sold for so great a price, and the native wild sheep, which inhabits the tops of the highest mountains. It attains the size of a large goat; the head resembles that of an ordinary sheep, but is furnished with strong, crooked horns: the skin and form of the body are like the reindeer, and it feeds chiefly on moss. It is fleet and active, achieving, like the chamois, prodigious springs among the rocks and precipices, and is, consequently, with difficulty killed or taken. In preparing for these leaps, its eye measures the distance with surprising accuracy; the animal then contracts its legs, and darts forward head-foremost to the destined spot, where it alights upon its feet, nor is it ever known to miss, although the point may be so small as to admit its four feet only by their being closely pressed together. The manner in which it balances itself after such leaps is also admirable: our ballet-dancers would consider it a model of a perfect *à plomb*. The monster of the antediluvian world, the mammoth, must have been an inhabitant of this country, since many of its bones have been found here.

The forests of Kamtschatka are not enlivened by singing-birds; indeed land-birds are all scarce; but there are infinite numbers of waterfowl of many species. Immense flocks of them are to be seen upon the lakes, rivers, morasses, and even the sea itself, in the vicinity of the shore. Fish is abundant, especially in the months of June and July. A single draught of the net provided us with as many as the whole crew could consume in several days. A sort of salmon, ling, and herrings, are preferred for winter stock; the latter, dried in the air, supply food for the dogs.

Kamtschatka was discovered in the year 1696, by a Cossack of Yakutsh, by name Luca Semenoff, who, on a report being spread of the existence of this country, set out with sixteen companions to make a journey hither. In the following years, similar expeditions were repeated in greater force, till Kamtschatka was subjected and made tributary to the Russian crown. The conquest of this country cost many Russian lives; and from the ferocity of the conquerors, and the difficulty of maintaining discipline amongst troops so scattered, ended in nearly exterminating the Kamtschatkans. Although subsequent regulations restrained the disorders of the wild Cossacks, the population is still very thin; but under a wise and careful government it will certainly increase.

The name of Kamtschatka, pronounced Kantschatka, conferred by the Russians, was adopted from the native appellation of the great river flowing through the country. This river derived its name, according to tradition, from Kontschat, a warrior of former times, who had a stronghold on its banks. It is strange that the Kamtschatkans had no designation either for themselves or their country. They called themselves simply men, as considering themselves either the only inhabitants of the earth, or so far surpassing all others, as to be alone worthy of this title. On the southern side of the peninsula, the aborigines are believed to have been distinguished by the name of Itelmen; but the signification of this word remains uncertain.

The Kamtschatkans acknowledged an Almighty Creator of the world, whom they called Kutka. They supposed that he inhabited the heavens; but had at one time dwelt in human form in Kamtschatka, and was the original parent of their race. Even here the tradition of a universal deluge prevails, and a spot is still shown, on the top of a mountain where Kutka landed from a boat, in order to replenish the world with men. The proverbial phrase current in Kamtschatka, to express a period long past, is, "that was in Kutka's days."

Before the expeditions of the Russians to Kamtschatka, the inhabitants were acquainted only with the neighbouring Koriacks and Tchuktchi.

They had also acquired some knowledge of Japan, from a Japanese ship wrecked on their coast. They acknowledged no chief, but lived in perfect independence, which they considered as their highest good.

Besides the supreme God Kutka, they had a host of inferior deities, installed by their imaginations in the forests, the mountains, and the floods. They adored them when their wishes were fulfilled, and insulted them when their affairs went amiss; like the lower class of Italians, who, when any disaster befalls them, take off their cap, enumerate into it as many saints' names as they can call to mind, and then trample it under foot. Two wooden household deities, Aschuschok and Hontai, were held in particular estimation. The former, in the figure of a man, officiated in scaring away the forest spirits from the house; for which service he was remunerated in food, his head being daily anointed with fish-soup. Hontai was half man, half fish, and on every anniversary of the purification from sin, a new one was introduced and placed beside his predecessors, so that the accumulated number of Hontais showed how many years the inhabitants had occupied their house.

The Kamtschatkans believed in their own immortality, and in that of the brute creation; but they expected in a future state to depend upon their labour for subsistence, as in the present life; they only hoped that the toil would be lightened, and its reward more abundant, that they might never suffer hunger. This idea of itself sufficiently proves, that the fisheries sometimes fail in their produce.

The several races of Kamtschatkans frequently waged war with each other; caused either by the forcible abduction of the women, or a deficiency in hospitality on their occasional interchange of visits, which was considered an insult to the guest, demanding a bloody revenge.

Their wars were seldom carried on openly; they preferred stratagem and artifice; and the conquerors practised the greatest cruelties on the conquered. If a party was so beleaguered as to lose all hope of effectual resistance, or of securing their safety by flight, knowing that no mercy would await a surrender, their warlike spirit did not desert them; they first murdered their women and children, and then rushed furiously on the enemy, to sell their lives as dearly as possible. Their weapons were lances, and bows and poisoned arrows.

To treat a guest with the utmost politeness, and leave no cause for hostility, the host was expected to heat his subterranean dwelling till it became almost insupportable: both parties then cast off all their attire, an enormous quantity of food was placed before the guest, and the fire was continually fed. When the visitor declared that he could no longer eat, or endure the heat of the place, all that courtesy required had been done, and the host expected a present in return for his hospitality.

At such entertainments the moucho-more, a deleterious species of mushroom, was usually introduced, as a mode of intoxication. Taken in small quantities, it is said to excite an agreeable hilarity of spirits; but if immoderately used, it will produce insanity of several days' duration. Animated by these enjoyments, the host and guests found mutual amusement in the exercise of their peculiar talent of mimicking men and animals.

The children when grown up showed little affection for their parents, neglected them in old age, and did not even consider it a violation of filial duty to kill them when they became burdensome. They also murdered their defective or weakly children, to spare them the misery of a languishing existence. They did not bury their dead, but dragged the corpse into the open air, by a thong tied about the neck, and left it a prey to dogs; under the belief, that those devoured by these animals, would in another world be drawn by the best dogs.

The mode of solemnizing marriages among the Kamtschatkans was tedious, and, on the part of the bridegroom, attended with many difficulties. A man who wished to marry a girl went to the house of her parents, and without farther declaration took his share in the domestic labours. He thus became the servant of the family, and was obliged to obey all their behests, till he succeeded in winning the favour of the girl and her parents. This might continue for years, and even in the end he was liable to be dismissed, without any compensation for his trouble. If, however, the maiden was pleased, and the parents were satisfied with him, they gave him permission to catch his beloved; from this moment the girl took all possible pains to avoid being alone with him, defended herself with a fishing-net and numerous girdles, all which were to be cut through with a stone knife, while all the family were upon the watch to rescue her at the first outcry: the unfortunate lover had probably no sooner laid hands upon his bride than he was seized by her relations, beaten, and dragged away by his hair; yet was he compelled to conquer and overpower her resistance, or to continue in unrewarded servitude. When, however, the catching was accomplished, the fair one herself proclaimed the victory, and the marriage was celebrated.

The present Kamtschatkans are an extremely good-natured, hospitable, timid people; in colour and features nearly resembling the Chinese and Japanese. They all profess the Christian religion; but secretly retain many of their heathen customs, particularly that of killing their deformed children.

The town, or rather village, adjoining the harbour of St. Peter and St. Paul, where the present Governor of Kamtschatka, Captain Stanizky, resides, though the principal place in the peninsula, contains but few convenient houses. The rest, about fifty in number, are mere huts, irregularly scattered up the side of a mountain. The inhabitants of this place, which bears the same name as the harbour, are all Russians, officers of the crown, sailors, disbanded soldiers, and some insignificant traders.

The Kamtschatkans live inland in little villages on the banks of the rivers, but seldom on the sea-coast.

From Krusenstern's representation, Kamtschatka appears very little altered in five-and-twenty years. The only advance made in that period, consists in the cultivation of potatoes by the inhabitants of St. Peter and St. Paul, and the entire water-carriage of various goods and necessaries of life, which were formerly needlessly enhanced in price by being brought overland, through Siberia to Ochotsk.

The northern part of the peninsula and the adjoining country, even to the icy sea, is inhabited by the Tschuktschi, a warlike nomad tribe, removing with celerity from place to place by means of their reindeer. They were not so easily conquered as the Kamtschatkans, and for five-and-thirty years incessantly annoyed the Russians, to whom they now only pay a small tribute in skins. Our cannon at length forced a peace upon them, which had not been long concluded, before there was reason to apprehend a breach of its conditions on their part, and an ambassador was sent to their Tajon, or chief, to discover their intentions. The chief drew a long knife from a sheath at his side, presented it to the ambassador, making him observe that it had a broken point, and addressed him as follows: "When my father died he gave me this knife, saying, 'My son, I received this broken knife from my uncle, whom I succeeded in the dignity of Tajon, and I promised him never to sharpen it against the Russians, because we never prosper in our combats with them; I therefore enjoin thee also to enter into no strife with them till this knife shall of itself renew its point.' You see that the knife is still edgeless, and my father's last will is sacred to me."

According to an accurate census taken of the population of Kamtschatka in the year 1822, it amounts, with the exception of the Tschuktschi, who cannot be computed, to two thousand four hundred and fifty-seven persons of the male, and one thousand nine hundred and forty-one of the female sex. Of these, the native Kamtschatkans were only one thousand four hundred and twenty-eight males, and one thousand three hundred and thirty females; the rest were Koriaks and Russians. They possessed ninety-one horses, seven hundred and eighteen head of cattle, three thousand eight hundred and forty-one dogs, and twelve thousand reindeer, the latter belonging exclusively to the Koriaks.

Unimportant as was the place where we now landed, a change is always agreeable after a long voyage; and the kind and hospitable reception we met with from the commander as well as the inhabitants, contributed greatly to our enjoyments.

We were gratified with a bear-hunt, which produced much sport, and gave us the satisfaction of killing a large and powerful bear. This animal is very numerous here, and is consequently easily met with by a hunting-party. The usually timid Kamtschatkan attacks them with the greatest courage. Often armed only with a lance and a knife, he endeavours to provoke the bear to the combat; and when it rises on its hind legs for defence or attack, the hunter rushes forward, and, resting one end of the lance on the ground, plunges the other into its breast, finally dispatching it with his knife. Sometimes, however, he fails in the attempt, and pays for his temerity with his life.

The following anecdote evinces the hardihood of the bears. Fish, which forms their chief nourishment, and which they procure for themselves from the rivers, was last year excessively scarce. A great famine consequently existed among them, and instead of retiring to their dens, they wandered about the whole winter through, even in the streets of St. Peter and St. Paul. One of them finding the outer gate of a house open, entered, and the gate accidentally closed after him. The woman of the house had just placed a large tea-machine,[1] full of boiling water, in the court, the bear smelt to it and burned his nose; provoked at the pain, he vented all his fury upon the kettle, folded his fore-paws round it, pressed it with his whole strength against his breast to crush it, and burnt himself, of course, still more and more. The horrible growl which rage and pain forced from him, brought all the inhabitants of the house and neighbourhood to the spot, and poor bruin was soon dispatched by shots from the windows. He has, however, immortalized his memory, and become a proverb amongst the town's people, for when any one injures himself by his own violence, they call him "the bear with the tea-kettle."

On the 14th of July, M. Preuss observed an eclipse of the sun, from which he determined the geographical longitude of St. Peter and St. Paul to be 201° 10' 31". On the same day Dr. Siegwald and Messrs. Lenz and Hoffman happily achieved the Herculean task of climbing the Owatscha Mountain, which lies near the harbour. Its height, according to barometrical measurement, is seven thousand two hundred feet. An intermittent smoke arose from its crater, and a cap let down a few feet within it was drawn up burnt. The gentlemen brought back with them some pieces of crystallized sulphur, as evidence of their having really pursued their examination quite into the mouth of the crater.

After having delivered all the articles which we had taken in for Kamtschatka, we left the harbour of St. Peter and St. Paul on the morning of the 20th of July, and with favouring breezes sailed for the Russian settlement of New Archangel, on the north-west coast of America.

At sunset the majestic mountains of Kamtschatka appeared for the last time within our horizon, and at a vast distance. This despised and desolate country may perhaps one day become a Russian Mexico. The only treasure of which we robbed it was, a swallow's nest! I mention it, because it long supplied the whole ship's company with amusement.

In the harbour of St. Peter and St. Paul, there is sufficient depth of water close to the shore to admit of landing by means of a plank only. This proximity led a pair of swallows to mistake our frigate for a building upon terra-firma, and to the infinite delight of the sailors, who regarded it as a lucky omen, they deliberately built themselves a nest close to my cabin. Undisturbed by the noise in the ship, the loving pair hatched their brood in safety, fed their young ones with the tenderest care, and cheered them with joyous songs. But when on a sudden they saw their peaceful dwelling removing from the land, they seemed astonished, and hovered anxiously about the ship, yet still fetched food for their young from the shore, till the distance became too great.

The struggle between the instincts of self-preservation and parental love then became perceptible. They flew round the vessel, then vanished for awhile, then suddenly returned to their hungry family, and stretching their open beaks towards them, seemed to lament that no food was to be found. This alternate disappearing and returning continued some time, and terminated in the parents returning no more; the sailors then took on themselves the care of the deserted orphans. They removed them from the nest where the parents warmth was necessary, to another lined with cotton, and fixed in a warm place, and fed them with flies, which seemed to please their palates very well. The system at first appeared to have perfectly succeeded, and we were in hopes of carrying them safely to America; when, in spite of the most careful attention, they fell sick, and on the eighth day, to the general sorrow, not one of our nurslings remained alive.

They however afforded an additional proof how kindly the common people of Russia are interested in all that is helpless.

NEW ARCHANGEL

THE swallows brought us no good fortune. The very day after we left Kamtschatka, one of our best sailors fell from the mast-head into the scuttle, and immediately expired. He had climbed thither in safety in the most violent storms, and executed the most difficult tasks with ease; now, in fine weather, on a tranquil sea, he met this fate.

These accidents happen most frequently to the best and cleverest sailors: they confide too much in their own ability, and consider too little the risks they run. It is impossible to warn them sufficiently.

This fatal accident produced a general melancholy among us, which the cloudy, wet, cold weather we soon encountered perpetually increased, till we reached the coast of America. Fortunately, we had all the time a strong west wind; by its help we passed the southern coasts of the Aleutian Islands, and on the 7th of August already approached the American coast. On this day the sun once more smiled on us; the sky afterwards continued clear, and the air became milder and pleasanter as we neared the land.

From our noon observation we were in latitude 55° 36', and longitude 140° 56'. In this region, some navigators have imagined they observed a regular current to the north; but our experience does not confirm the remark. A current carried us from twenty to thirty miles in twenty-four hours, setting sometimes north, and sometimes south, according to the impulse of the wind; close to shore only the current is regularly to the north. The inhabitants concurred in this observation.

We now steered direct for the bay called by the English Norfolk Sound, and by the Russians Sitka Bay, and the island at its back, which the natives call Sitchachan, whence the Russian Sitka. This island, called by the Russians New Archangel, is at present the principal settlement of the Russian-American company.

On the morning of the 9th of August, we were, according to my calculation, near land; but a thick fog concealed us from every object so much as fifty fathoms distant. At length the mid-day sun burst forth, and rapidly dispelling the curtain of cloud and fog, surprised us with a view of the American coast. We were standing right for the mouth of the above-mentioned bay, at a small distance from the Edgecumbe promontory; a table-land so elevated, that in clear weather it serves for a safe landmark at a distance of fifty miles.

We were all day prevented by a calm from making the bay, and were obliged to content ourselves with admiring the wild high rocky coast, with its fir forests. Though now in a much higher latitude than in Kamtschatka, we yet saw no snow, even on the summits of the highest mountains; a proof of the superior mildness of the climate on the American, compared with the Asiatic coast.

The next day we took advantage of a light wind blowing towards the bay; but so gloomy was the weather, that we could scarcely see land, and not one of our crew had ever been in the bay before. It stretches from the entrance to New Archangel twenty-five miles in length, and is full of small islands and shallows; a pilot was not to be thought of; but we happily overcame all our difficulties. We tacked through all the intricacies of this navigation amidst heavy rain and a thick gloom, till we dropped the anchor within musket-shot of the fortress.

We here found the frigate Kreissac, under the command of Captain Lasaref, sent here by Government for the protection of trade, and whom we were destined to succeed.

The appearance of a vessel of our native country, in so distant and desolate a corner of the earth, naturally produced much joy amongst our people. I immediately paid a visit to Captain Lasaref, and then to the Governor of the Colony, Captain Murawief, an old acquaintance, whom I had not seen for many years. At so great a distance from home, friendships are quickly formed between compatriots, even if previously unknown to each other,—how much then must their interest increase, when long ago cemented in the native land! My intercourse with this gentleman, equally distinguished for his noble character and cultivated mind, conduced much to the comfort of a tedious residence in this desert.

To my enquiry, whether my vessel must now remain stationary at the colony, he replied, that until the first of March of the following year (1825), my time was at my own disposal, but that after that period my presence could not be dispensed with. I therefore proceeded to visit California and the Sandwich Islands, and returned to New Archangel on the 23rd of February 1825.

The nearer we drew to the land the milder the weather became, and we were astonished, in so northern a country, to see the mountains at this season of the year entirely free from snow to a considerable height. Throughout this winter, however, which had been particularly mild, the snow in many of the vallies had never lain above a few hours together. Here, under fifty-seven degrees north latitude, the climate is much milder than in European countries similarly situated; as again the north-east coast of Asia is much colder than countries of an equal latitude in Europe.

On the morning of the 24th, after passing a stormy night on this dangerous coast, we happily succeeded in reaching the harbour, and anchoring before the fortress, just before another and most violent tempest set in.

We were received with great rejoicing; and on the following day placed the frigate in such a position, and at such a distance from the fortress, as was most convenient to accomplish the purpose of our mission. To explain this, we must take a short review of the Russian settlement here, and of the affairs of the original inhabitants.

From the highest antiquity to the present day, examples are not wanting of men trusting themselves in small and frail vessels to the perils of the ocean, and performing astonishing voyages, without any of those aids which the improvements in science and mechanical art place within our reach. The children of the Sun in Peru, and the founders of the regular political constitution which existed in Mexico before its invasion by the Spaniards, probably floated in little canoes over the trackless surface of the ocean, as the inhabitants of the South Sea Islands do to this day.

The voyages of the Phœnicians and Romans are sufficiently known; as are those of the Norman heroes who discovered Greenland, Iceland, and even North America.

In vessels just as defective, destitute of the instruments requisite for observing their course, and of any fixed notion concerning the conformation or extent of the earth, often even without a compass, ignorant Russian adventurers have embarked from Ochotsk, and rounding Kamtschatka, have discovered the Aleutian Islands, and attained to the north-west coast of America. Year after year, in more numerous parties, they repeated these expeditions, tempted by the beautiful furs which were procured in the newly-discovered countries. Many of their vessels were lost,—many of those who ventured in them were attacked and murdered by savages; yet still new adventurers were found yearly encountering all these risks, for the sake of the profitable traffic in these furs, especially that of the sea-otter. By degrees they formed themselves into commercial societies, which obtained a firmer footing on the Aleutian Islands, and even on the northern parts of the western coast of America, carried on a regular trade to Siberia, but lived in a state of continual violence and dissensions.

Superior to the natives by the possession of fire-arms, they became overbearing, treated the timid Aleutians in the most cruel manner, and would perhaps have quite exterminated them, had not the Emperor Paul interposed. By his order, in 1797, a Russian-American mercantile company was established, which was to supersede the trading societies hitherto existing, and possess the exclusive privilege of carrying on trade and founding settlements in these regions. The directors, in whose hands was vested the administration of the affairs and appointment of the governor of these settlements, were to reside in Petersburg, under the control of the government, to which they were responsible.

At first the sea-otters were plentiful, even on the coast of Kamtschatka; but the unlimited pursuit of them diminished their numbers so rapidly, that the Company was obliged to extend their search for them over the Aleutian Islands, and even to the island of Kodiack, lying on the American coast, where they had fixed their chief settlement.

From thence the chase was continued to the bay of Tschugatsk and Cook's river. The poor otters were severe sufferers, for the beauty of the skin nature had bestowed on them. They were pursued in every possible direction, and such numbers annually killed, that at length they became scarce, even in these quarters, having already almost wholly disappeared from Kamtschatka and the Aleutian Islands.

The Company therefore resolved to extend their settlements farther south; and thus, in the year 1804, arose the colony on the island of Sitka, whose natives call themselves after their island, but are styled by the Russians Kalushes.

The island is only separated from the mainland by a narrow inlet of the sea. It extends over three degrees and a half of latitude; and, in fact, consists of three islands, as I ascertained by personal examination in boats. The channels, however, which separate them are so narrow, that the three might easily pass for one. The coast of Sitka Bay is intersected by many deep creeks, and the neighbouring waters thickly sprinkled with little rocky islands overgrown with wood, which are a protection against storms, and present a strong wall of defence against the waves.

The harbour of New Archangel is equally well defended by nature, and needs no assistance from art.

A bold enterprising man of the name of Baronof, long superintended the Company's establishments. Peculiarly adapted by nature for the task of contending with a wild people, he seemed to find a pleasure in the occupation. Although the conquest of the Sitkaens, or Kalushes, was not so easily achieved as that of the more timid Aleutians and Kodiacks, he finally accomplished it. A warlike, courageous, and cruel race, provided with fire-arms by the ships of the North American United States, in exchange for otters' skins, maintained an obstinate struggle against the invaders. But Baronof at length obtained a decisive superiority over them. What he could not obtain by presents, he took by force, and, in spite of all opposition, succeeded in founding the settlement on this island. He built some dwelling-houses, made an entrenchment, and having, in his own opinion, appeased the Kalushes by profuse presents, confided the new conquest to a small number of Russians and Aleutians. For a short time matters went on prosperously, when suddenly, the garrison left by Baronof, believing itself in perfect safety, was attacked one night by great numbers of Kalushes, who entered the entrenchments without opposition, and murdered all they met there with circumstances of atrocious cruelty. A few Aleutians only, who happened to be out in their little baidars,[2] escaped by standing out to sea, and brought to Kodiack the news of the annihilation of the settlement at Sitka.

This occurrence took place in the year 1804, when the present Admiral Krusenstern made his voyage round the world, and his second ship, the Neva, was bound for this colony. Baronof immediately seized so excellent an opportunity for revenging himself on the Kalushes. He armed three vessels, and sailed in company with the Neva to Sitka. When the Kalushes heard that the warrior Nonok, as they called Baronof, had returned, terror prevented their attempting to oppose his landing; and they retired in great haste to their fortification, consisting of a great quadrangle closely set round with thick, high beams, broken only by one very small and strong door. The pallisadoes were furnished with loop-holes, for the firing of muskets and falconets, with which the besieged were amply supplied. This wooden fortress, enclosing about three hundred fighting men with their families, held out several days; but no sooner had the heavy guns of the Russians effected a breach, than the besieged, finding their position no longer tenable, surrendered at discretion, and delivered over the sons of their chiefs as hostages for their submission.

Though peace was now established, and they were allowed to retire unmolested, yet, mistrusting the Russians, they stole away secretly in a dark night, having first murdered all who, whether from age or infancy, might be burdensome to them in their flight. Morning discovered the cruelty perpetrated by these barbarians, who, in their fears, judged the Russians by themselves. From this time Baronof remained nominally in possession of the island, and actually of a hill upon it forming a natural fortification, and formerly inhabited by a chief of the Kalushes called Katelan.

The savages thirsted for revenge; and, notwithstanding the treaties concluded with them, unceasingly sought to gratify it by secret arts and ambushes; so that the Russians, unless well armed, and in considerable numbers, could not venture beyond the shelter of their fortress without the most imminent danger of being murdered.

Baronof re-founded the settlement, and having strengthened by scientific defences the high hill, which falls on every side in abrupt precipices, has rendered it perfectly safe from every attack. The necessary dwelling-houses were soon erected; and this place, under the name of New Archangel, became the capital of the Russian possessions in America, stretching from 52° of latitude to the Icy Sea, and including also two settlements lying farther south, of which I shall hereafter have occasion to speak.

Baronof himself resided from this time in New Archangel, and the chase of the sea-otters proved very advantageous to the Company; but so scarce are these animals now become, even here, that the numbers caught only suffice to cover the expenses of maintaining a force sufficient for protection against the savages. For this reason, the Company have contemplated the necessity of entirely abandoning the settlement at New Archangel, and making Kodiack once more their capital. It were, however, a pity this plan should be adopted, as it would afford facilities to other nations, by settling in these regions, to disturb the trade of the Company. But the Company may possibly be compelled to give up New Archangel, by their resources not permitting them to retain it, unless they should receive some assistance from Government.

The climate of Sitka is not so severe as might have been expected from its latitude. In the middle of winter the cold is not excessive, and never lasts long. Agriculture notwithstanding does not appear to be successful here. There is not perhaps a spot in the world where so much rain falls; a dry day is a perfect rarity, and this would itself account for the failure of corn; the nature of the ground is however equally inimical to it.

There are no plains of any extent; the small valleys being every where surrounded by high steep rocks of granite, and consequently overshadowed the greater part of the day. Some vegetables, such as cabbages, turnips, and potatoes, prosper very well: the latter are raised even by the Kalushes, who have learned from the Russians the manner of cultivating them, and consider them as a great delicacy. Upon the continent of America, the climate, under the same latitude, is said to be incomparably better than on this island, although the cold is rather more severe. Great plains are there to be met with, where wheat could probably be successfully cultivated.

The forests of Sitka, consisting principally of fir and beech, are lofty and thick. Some of their trees are a hundred and sixty feet in height, and from six to seven feet in diameter. From these noble trunks the Kalushes form their large canoes, which sometimes carry from twenty-five to thirty men. They are laboriously and skilfully constructed; but the credit their builders may claim for this one branch of industry is nearly all that belongs to a barbarous and worthless race of men.

Wild and unfruitful as this country appears, the soil is rich, so that its indigenous plants, of which there are no great variety, attain a very large growth. Several kinds of berries, particularly raspberries and black currants, of an enormous size but watery taste, are met with in considerable quantities.

The sea, near the coast and in the bays, abounds in fish and in mammalia. Whales, sea-hogs, seals, sea-lions, &c. are very numerous; but of the fish, which chiefly afford subsistence both to the natives and the Russians, the best are herrings, salmon, and cod, of which there is a superfluity. There is no great variety of birds native to this coast; but the beautiful white-headed eagle, and several sorts of pretty humming-birds, migrate from warmer climates to build their nests in Sitka. It is extraordinary that these tender little creatures, always inhabiting hot countries, should venture thus far northwards.

Among the quadrupeds frequenting the forests is the black bear, whose skin fetches so high a price in Russia, and a species of wild sheep known to us only by the descriptions of the Kalushes, and in which our natural histories are still deficient. It differs greatly from that of Kamtschatka: its wool rivals silk in the delicacy and softness of its texture. The most remarkable animal, however, is the sea-otter, that which has allured merchants hither from distant countries, and which, if such intercourse should improve the morals and intellects of the natives, may be considered as their benefactor. This animal inhabits only the north-west coast of America, between the latitudes of 30° and 60°, in smaller numbers the Aleutian islands, and formerly the coast of Kamtschatka and the Kurile islands. Its skin makes the finest fur in the world, and is as highly prized by the Chinese as by the Europeans. Its value advances yearly, with the increasing scarceness of the animal; it will soon entirely disappear, and exist only in description to decorate our zoological works.

Attempts have been made to identify the sea and river otter, because there is a considerable resemblance in their form; but the skin of the former is without comparison finer than the latter, which inhabits only lakes and rivers, where the sea-otter is never found.

They are often seen on the surface of the water, many miles from land, lying asleep on their backs, with their young, of which only two are produced at a birth, lying over them sucking. The young cannot swim till they are some months old; but the mother, when she goes out to sea in search of food, carries them on her back and brings them back to her hole in the rocks, when she has satisfied her hunger. If seen by the hunter during these excursions, she is a certain prey, for she never forsakes her offspring however they embarrass her swimming, but, in common with the male, defends them courageously against every attack.

The lungs of these animals are so constructed that they cannot subsist for more than a few minutes under water, but are necessitated to re-ascend to the surface for breath. These opportunities are seized by the hunters, who would seldom succeed, if the otter could remain long under water, where it swims with great rapidity and skill. Even with the above advantage, the chase is very toilsome, and sometimes dangerous. It is carried on in the following manner.

The hunters row in the little Aleutian baidars round the coast, and for some miles out to sea, provided with bows, arrows, and short javelins. As soon as they see an otter they throw their javelins, or shoot their arrows. The animal is seldom struck; it immediately dives, and as it swims very rapidly, the skill of the hunter is displayed in giving the baidar the same direction as that taken by the animal. As soon as the otter re-appears on the water, it is again fired at, when it dives again; and the pursuit is continued in the same way till the creature becomes so weary that it is easily struck.

They tear out with their teeth the arrows which wound them; and often, especially if their young are with them, boldly fall upon the canoes and attack their persecutors with teeth and claws; these conflicts however uniformly end in the defeat and death of the otter. The more baidars are in company, the safer is the hunt, but with experienced hunters two are enough. They often encounter great perils by venturing out too far to sea, and being overtaken by storms.

I now proceed, though with some reluctance, to the description of the natives, the Kalushes. They are, as I have already said, the most worthless people on the face of the earth, and disgusting to such a degree that I must beg fastidious readers to pass over a few pages. The truth of my narrative makes it necessary for me to submit to the revolting task of showing to what point of degradation human nature may sink.

The Sitka Islanders, as well as their neighbours on the continent, are large and strongly built, but have their limbs so ill-proportioned, that they all appear deformed. Their black, straight hair hangs dishevelled over their broad faces, their cheek-bones stand out, their noses are wide and flat, their mouths large, their lips thick, their eyes small, black, and fiery, and their teeth strikingly white.

Their natural colour is not very dark; but they appear much more so than is natural to them, from the custom of smearing themselves daily over the face and body with ochre and a sort of black earth. Immediately after the birth, the head of the child is compressed, to give it what they consider a fine form, in which the eyebrows are drawn up, and the nostrils stretched asunder. In common with many other nations, they tear the beard out by the roots as soon as it appears. This is the business of the women. Their usual clothing consists of a little apron; but the rich wear blankets, purchased from the Russians, or from the American ships, and tied by two corners round the neck, so that they hang down and cover the back. Some of them wear bear-skins in a similar manner. The most opulent possess some European garments, which they wear on great occasions, and which would have an absurd effect were they not so disgusting as to extinguish all inclination to laugh. They never cover the head but in heavy rain, and then protect it by round caps of grass, so ingeniously and closely plaited as to exclude every drop of water.

Whatever the degree of heat or cold, they never vary their costume; and I believe there is not a people in the world so hardened against the weather. In the winter, during a cold of 10° of Reaumur, the Kalushes walk about naked, and jump into the water as the best method of warming themselves. At night they lie without any covering, under the open sky, near a great fire, so near indeed as to be sometimes covered by the hot ashes. The women whom I have seen were either dressed in linen shifts reaching to their feet, or in plaited mats.

The custom common to both sexes, of painting their faces in broad, black, white, and red stripes crossed in all directions, gives them a peculiarly wild and savage appearance. Although this painting is quite arbitrary, and subject to no exact rules, the different races distinguish each other by it. To give the face a yet more insane cast, their long, hanging, tangled hair is mixed with the feathers of the white eagle. When powdered and painted in this way, the repulsiveness of the Kalush women, by nature excessively ugly, may be imagined; but they have a method of still farther disfiguring themselves. As soon as they are nearly marriageable, an incision is made in the under-lip, and a bone passed through it, which is exchanged from time to time for a thicker one, that the opening may be continually widened. At length a sort of double button, of an oval form, called a kaluga, which, among the people of rank, is often four inches long, and three broad, is forced in so as to make the under lip stand forward thus much in a horizontal direction, and leave the lower teeth quite bare. The outer rim of the lip surrounding the wooden button becomes by the violent stretching as thin as a packthread, and of a dark blue colour.

In running, the lip flaps up and down so as to knock sometimes against the chin and sometimes against the nose. Upon the continent, the kaluga is worn still larger; and the female who can cover her whole face with her under-lip passes for the most perfect beauty. Men and women pierce the gristle of the nose, and stick quills, iron rings, and all kinds of ornaments, through it. In their ears, which are also pierced in many places, they wear strings of bones, muscle-shells, and beads.

It would be difficult to convey an adequate idea of the hideousness of these people when their costume is thus complete; but the lips of the women, held out like a trough, and always filled with saliva stained with tobacco-juice, of which they are immoderately fond, is the most abominably revolting part of the spectacle.

The Kalushes have no fixed residence, but hover round the coast in their large canoes, which they call the women's, carrying all their property with them. When they fix upon any spot for their temporary establishment, they build a hut with great celerity, having all the materials at hand. They drive a number of stakes into the ground in a quadrangular form, fill the interstices with thin planks, and roof in the whole with the bark of trees. With such a dwelling they are satisfied; in the severest winter the family sit in a circle, carrying on their several employments round a fire in the centre. The interior displays as much filthiness as if the inhabitants belonged to the dirtiest class of the brute creation. The smoke; the stench of bad fish, and blubber; the repulsive figures of the women, disgustingly occupied in seeking for vermin on the heads or skins of the men, and actually *eating them* when found; the great utensil for the service of the whole family, which is also the only vessel capable of containing water to wash with; all this soon drives the most inquisitive European out of so detestable a den.

Their food, sufficiently disgusting in itself, is rendered still more so by their manner of eating. It consists almost exclusively of fish, of which the whale is the chief favourite, and its blubber an especial dainty. This is sometimes cooked upon red-hot stones, but more commonly eaten raw. The skins of the sea-otters form their principal wealth, and are a substitute for money; these they barter with the ships which trade with them, to the prejudice of the Russian Company, for muskets, powder, and lead. No Kalush is without one musket at least, of which he perfectly understands the use. The richer a Kalush is, the more powerful he becomes; he has a multitude of wives who bring him a numerous family, and he purchases male and female slaves who must labour and fish for him, and strengthen his force when engaged in warfare. These slaves are prisoners of war, and their descendants; the master's power over them is unlimited, and he even puts them to death without scruple. When the master dies, two of his slaves are murdered on his grave, that he may not want attendance in the other world; these are chosen long before the event occurs, but meet the destiny that awaits them, very philosophically. The continual wars which the different races carry on against each other, with a ferocious cruelty uncommon even among savages, may account for the scanty population of this district; the fire-arms with which, to their own misfortune, they have been furnished by the American ships, have contributed to render their combats more bloody, and consequently to cause renewed and increased irritation. Bows and arrows were formerly their only weapons; now, besides their muskets, they have daggers, and knives half a yard long; they never attack their enemies openly, but fall suddenly upon them in moments of the utmost fancied security. The hope of booty, or of taking a prisoner, is a sufficient motive for one of these treacherous attacks, in which they practise the greatest barbarities; hence the Kalushes, even in time of peace, are always on their guard. They establish their temporary abodes on spots in some measure fortified by nature, and commanding an extensive view on all sides. During the night, the watch is confided to women, who, assembled round a fire outside the hut, amuse themselves by recounting the warlike deeds of their husbands and sons.

Domestic occupations, even the most laborious, are also left to females; the men employing themselves only in hunting, and building their canoes. The slaves are required to assist the women, who often treat them in a most merciless manner. The females take an active part in the wars; they not only stimulate the valour of the men, but even support them in the battle.

Besides the desire of booty, the most frequent occasion of warfare is revenge. One murder can only be atoned by another; but it is indifferent whether the murderer or one of his relations fall,—the custom merely requires a man for a man; should the murdered person be a female, a female is required in return. A case which would appear inconceivable has actually occurred,—that one of these most disgusting creatures has occasioned a struggle similar to that of Troy for the fair Helen, and an advantageous peace has been obtained by the cession of one of these monsters. The Kalush, who would probably look coldly on our most lovely females, finds his filthy countrywomen, with their lip-troughs, so charming, that they often awaken in him the most vehement passion. In proof of this, I remember an occurrence which took place during our residence in Sitka, among a horde of Kalushes who had encamped in the vicinity of the fortress. A girl had four lovers, whose jealousy produced the most violent quarrels: after fighting a long time without any result, they determined to end the strife by murdering the object of their love, and the resolution was immediately executed with their lances. The whole horde assembled round the funeral pile, and chanted a song, a part of which was interpreted by one of our countrymen, who had been long resident here. "Thou wast too beautiful—thou couldst not live—men looked on thee, and madness fired their hearts!"

Savage as this action was, another exceeded it in ferocity. A father, irritated by the cries of his child, an infant in the cradle, snatched it up, and threw it into a vessel full of boiling whale-oil. These examples are sufficient to characterise this hateful people, who appear to be in every respect the very refuse of human nature.

Their weddings are celebrated merely by a feast given to the relatives of the bride. The dead are burned, and their ashes preserved in small wooden boxes, in buildings appropriated to that purpose. They have a confused notion of immortality, and this is the only trace of religion which appears amongst them. They have neither priests, idols, nor any description of worship, but they place great faith in witchcraft; and the sorcerers, who are also their physicians, are held in high estimation, though more feared than loved. These sorcerers profess to heal the sick by conjurations of the Wicked Spirit; they are, however, acquainted with the medicinal properties of many herbs, but carefully conceal their knowledge as a profitable mystery.

We often received visits on board from chiefs of the Kalushes, generally with their whole family and attendants, who came to examine the ship, receive presents, and eat their fill, expressing their gratitude for these civilities by attempting to entertain us with their horrid national dance. Before coming on board, they usually rowed several times round the ship, howling a song to the following effect: "We come to you as friends, and have really no evil intention. Our fathers lived in strife with you, but let peace be between us. Receive us with hospitality, and expect the same from us." This song was accompanied by a sort of tambourine, which did not improve its harmony. They would not climb the ship's side till we had several times repeated our invitation, as it is not their custom to accept the first offer of hospitality, probably from a feeling of distrust. On these visits, the Kalushes were more than usually particular in the decoration of their persons. Their faces were so thickly smeared with stripes of red, black, and white paint, that their natural colour could not be known. Their bodies were painted with black stripes, and their hair covered with a quantity of white down and feathers, which were scattered around with every motion of their heads. Ermine-skins are also frequently fastened into the hair. A wolf or bear-skin, or a blanket, tied round the neck, covers their bodies, and they use an eagle's wing or tail as a fan. Their feet are always bare.

When on such occasions they had seen all they wished of the ship, except the cabins, (for these I would not suffer them to enter, on account of the abominable stench left behind by the rancid oil and blubber, which they used as perfumes,) they assembled upon deck to dance. The women did not dance, but assisted as musicians. Their song, accompanied by the dull music of the tambourine, consisted of a few hollow and unconnected tones, sent forth at intervals to keep time with the stamping of their feet. The men made the most extraordinary motions with their arms and bodies, varying them by high leaps into the air, while showers of feathers fell from their heads. Every dancer retained his own place, but turning continually round and round, gave the spectators an opportunity of admiring him on all sides. One only stood a little apart; he was particularly decorated with ermine-skins and feathers, and beat time for the dancing with a staff ornamented with the teeth of the sea-otter. He appeared to be the director of all the movements.

At every pause we offered tobacco-leaves to the dancers and musical ladies: both sexes eagerly seized the favourite refreshment, and crammed their mouths with it, then recommencing the music and dancing with renewed alacrity. When at length downright exhaustion put an end to the spectacle, the Kalushes were entertained with a favourite mess of rice boiled with treacle. They lay down round the wooden dishes, and helped themselves greedily with their dirty hands. During the meal, the women were much inconvenienced by their lip-troughs; the weight of the rice made them hang over the whole chin, and the mouth could not contain all that was intended for it.

During one of these repasts, the Kalushes were much terrified by a young bear which we had brought from Kamtschatka: breaking loose from his chain, he sprang over their heads, and seizing on the wooden vessel that contained the rice, carried it off in triumph. At parting we always gave them a dram of brandy, which they are very fond of, and can drink in considerable quantities without injury.

That no vice may be wanting to complete their characters, the Kalushes are great gamblers. Their common game is played with little wooden sticks painted of various colours, and called by several names, such as, crab, whale, duck, &c., which are mingled promiscuously together, and placed in heaps covered with moss; the players being then required to tell in which heap the crab, the whale, &c. lies. They lose at this game all their possessions, and even their wives and children, who then become the property of the winner.

During the whole of our residence at Sitka, we maintained peace with the Kalushes, which may be entirely attributed to the moderation and intrepidity of our sailors.

Opposite our frigate, on the shore, the ship's cooper had settled under a tent, almost all our casks being in want of repair; and I allowed him three armed sailors as assistants and protectors against the Kalushes.

One day ten of these savages armed with long knives came into the tent; having sat for some time contemplating the work, they became very troublesome, and, on being forbidden to pass the bounds previously prescribed, drew their knives and attacked the cooper, who would have been severely wounded had he not by good fortune parried a dangerous thrust. The three sailors now sprang forward with their loaded muskets; but as they had received the strictest injunctions not to shed blood, except in the most extreme necessity, they contented themselves with standing before the Kalushes and keeping them off with their bayonets. The savages at first continued to threaten the sailors, but on finding they were not to be intimidated, thought proper to retire to the forest. Had a skirmish really ensued, the consequences might have been serious. The Kalushes would all have united against us, and by rushing upon us from their hiding-places, whenever we left the protection of the ship or the fortress, might have done us much mischief. For this reason, Captain Murawieff, the governor of the settlement, had always exerted himself to the utmost to prevent any disputes. By his judicious regulations, he had acquired great influence over the natives, and had effected considerable improvement in their behaviour. In every respect, indeed, the administration of this excellent man has been such as to promote the true welfare of the colonies; and if the plans laid down by him for the future be adhered to, the trade of the Company will be materially benefited, and new sources of profit opened to them.

I have already mentioned that no people in the world surpass the citizens of the United States in the boldness, activity, and perseverance of their mercantile speculations. This observation was confirmed by an instance we met with here.

On the 16th of April 1825, a two-masted ship ran into this harbour from Boston. It had performed the voyage by Cape Horn in a hundred and sixty-six days, without having put into any intermediate port. Captain Blanchard, proprietor both of the ship, and of the whole cargo, had, upon the strength of a mere report, expended his whole capital upon certain articles of which he had heard that New Archangel was in need; and now, at the close of his immense voyage, found with dismay that not only was the colony well provided for the present, but that a ship was also daily expected from St. Petersburg laden with every thing it could desire. As, however, his offers were very reasonable, the ship and cargo were subsequently purchased of him for twenty-one thousand skins of sea-cats, (not otters) with the stipulation on his part, that he, his crew, and his skins, should be transported to the Sandwich Islands, whence he hoped to procure a passage for Canton, and there to dispose of his merchandise to advantage. These skins are usually sold in China for two Spanish dollars each.

On the arrival of Captain Blanchard's ship in port, the whole crew, he himself not excepted, were in a state of intoxication; and it appeared to be mere good luck that they had escaped the dangers of so many rocks and shallows; but the North Americans are such clever sailors, that even when drunk they are capable of managing a ship. It is also probable, that these had lived more soberly during the voyage, and had been tempted by the joy of completing it, to extraordinary indulgence. On my visit to the ship, I could not help remarking the great economy of all its arrangements: no such thing, for instance, as a looking-glass was to be seen, except the one kept for measuring the angle of the sextant, and that, small as it was, assisted the whole crew in the operation of shaving.

On the 30th of July, the ship Helena, belonging to the Company, arrived in New Archangel from Petersburg, bringing an ample provision of necessaries for the colony. To us this ship was particularly welcome, as the bearer of permission to leave our station and return to Russia. We immediately set to work to get our vessel in sailing order; and the 11th of August was the long wished-for day, when, favoured by a fresh north wind, we bade adieu to New Archangel, where we had passed five months and a-half surrounded by a people calculated only to inspire aversion, and without relief to the wearisomeness of our mode of life, except in the society of Captain Murawieff and the few Russian inhabitants of the fortress.

I determined to return to Kronstadt by the Chinese Sea and the Cape of Good Hope. But having no intention of following Captain Blanchard's example, in wearing out my crew by a voyage of unreasonable length without any relaxation, I appointed Manilla, in the Philippine island of Luçon, for their resting-place, after having made another attempt to find the Ralik chain of islands.

The medium of the astronomical observations made during these five months, gave, as the geographical longitude of New Archangel, 135° 33' 18", and the latitude as 57° 2' 57"; the declination of the needle as 27° 30' east. According to this, the promontory of Mount Edgecumbe is in the longitude 136° 1' 49"; consequently about 20' more westerly than appears on Vancouver's map.

We found a similar difference between our observation of St. Francisco and his; I therefore believe that his whole survey of the north-west coast of America represents it more easterly than it really is. Our longitudes have the greater claim to confidence, as they were the results of repeated observations on land, while his were merely taken on shipboard *en passant*.

The medium of our observations at New Archangel upon the difference in high tides at the new and full moon, gave thirty minutes for the time, and sixteen feet for the greatest difference in the height of the water.

CALIFORNIA, AND THE RUSSIAN SETTLEMENT OF ROSS

I HAVE already mentioned, in the foregoing chapter, that I was allowed to pass the winter of 1824 in California and the Sandwich Islands. Captain Lasaref also, whom I relieved on the station, proposed to run into St. Francisco on the coast of California, on his return, in order there to lay in fresh provisions for his passage round Cape Horn. He first awaited, however, the arrival of the post from St. Petersburg, which passes between these distant points of our far-spreading monarchy only once in the year, arriving in the spring at Ochotsk by the way of Siberia, and reaching New Archangel in the autumn by sea.

It was on the 10th of September 1824, that after having made the necessary preparations for our subsequent residence in New Archangel, and having properly equipped the ship, we again put to sea, and a brisk north wind soon carried us in a southerly direction towards the fertile peninsula of California. Our voyage was safe, and varied by no remarkable occurrence, except that under forty degrees of latitude we were indulged with the spectacle of a most extraordinary struggle between two opposing winds.

After a few days' pretty fresh breezes from the south, clouds suddenly appeared in the north, and, by the motion of the water, we perceived that an equally strong wind was rising in that direction. The waves from the opposite regions foamed and raged against each other like hostile forces; but between them lay a path some fathoms broad, and stretching from east to west to an immeasurable length, which appeared perfectly neutral ground, and enjoyed all the repose of the most profound peace, not a single breath troubling the glassy smoothness of its surface. After a time, victory declared for Boreas, and he drove the smooth strip towards our vessel, which had hitherto been sailing in the territory of the south wind. We presently entered the calm region; and while we had not a puff to swell our sails, the wind raged with undiminished fury on both sides. This strange spectacle lasted for about a quarter of an hour; when the north wind, which had been continually advancing, reached us, and carried us quickly forward towards the point of our destination.

On the 25th of September we found ourselves, by observations, in the neighbourhood of the promontory called by the Spaniards "the King," not far from the bay of St. Francisco; but a thick fog, which at this season always reigns over the coast of California, veiled the wished-for land till the

27th. At ten o'clock in the morning of this day, at a distance of only three miles, we doubled his rocky majesty, a high bold hill terminating towards the sea in a steep wall of black rock, and having nothing at all regal in its appearance,—and perceived in his neighbourhood a very strong surf, occasioned by two contrary and violent currents raging, with the vain fury of insurrection, against the tranquillity of his immoveable throne.

The channel leading into the beautiful basin of St. Francisco is only half gun-shot wide, and commanded by a fortress situated on its left bank, on a high rock, named after St. Joachim. We could distinguish the republican flag, the waving signal, that even this most northern colony of Spain no longer acknowledges the authority of the mother country; we also remarked a few cavalry and a crowd of people who were watching our swiftly sailing vessel with the most eager attention. As we drew nearer, a sentinel grasped with both hands a long speaking trumpet, and enquired our nation and from whence we came. This sharp interrogatory, the sight of the cannon pointed upon our track, and the military, few indeed, but ready for battle, might have induced an opinion that the fortress had power to refuse entrance even to a ship of war, had we not been acquainted with the true state of affairs. St. Joachim, on his rocky throne, is truly a very peaceable and well-disposed saint; no one of his cannon is in condition to fire a single shot, and his troops are cautious of venturing into actual conflict: he fights with words only. I would not therefore refuse to his fortress the courtesy of a salute, but was much astonished at not finding my guns returned. An ambassador from shore soon solved the mystery, by coming to beg so much powder as would serve to answer my civility with becoming respect.

As soon as we had dropped anchor, the whole of the military left the fortress without a garrison, to mingle with the assemblage of curious gazers on the shore, where the apparition of our ship seemed to excite as much astonishment as in the South Sea Islands. I now sent Lieutenant Pfeifer ashore, to notify our arrival in due form to the commandant, and to request his assistance in furnishing our vessel with fresh provisions. The commandant himself, Don Martinez Ignatio, lieutenant of cavalry, had been summoned to the capital Monterey, to attend Congress, and was absent; his deputy, the second lieutenant, Don Joseph Sanchez, received my envoy with much cordiality, and referred in a very flattering manner to my former visit to this port, in the ship Rurik. Don Sanchez was at that time a brave subaltern; but had since, under republican colours, risen in the service. He promised to lend us every assistance in his power, and proved his friendly intentions by an immediate present of fruits, vegetables, and fresh meats.

As our accounts of California are few and defective, a rapid glance at the history and constitution of this unknown but beautiful country, richly endowed by Nature with all that an industrious population could require to furnish the comforts and enjoyments of life, but hitherto sadly neglected under Spanish mis-government, will probably not be unwelcome to the readers who have accompanied me thus far: I will therefore, on its behalf, defer, for a short space, the account of our residence here.

The narrow peninsula on the north-west coast of America, beginning at St. Diego's Point, under thirty-two degrees of latitude, and ending with the promontory of St. Lucas, under twenty-two degrees, was first exclusively called California; but the Spaniards extended this appellation to their more recent discoveries on this coast towards the north; since which, the peninsula has been named Old, and the more northern coast to the Bay of St. Francisco, in thirty-seven degrees latitude, New California; from thence begins the so-called New Albion.

Mexico did not suffice to the ambition of its restless conqueror Cortez. To extend still farther the dominion of Spain, he directed the building of large vessels on the western coast of Mexico; and thus, in the year 1534, was California first seen by Spanish navigators, and in 1537 visited by Francisco de Ulloa. When information of the new discoveries reached the Spanish government, they resolved, contrary to their proceedings in the cases of Mexico and Peru, to gain peaceable possession of the new country by converting the inhabitants to the Christian religion, and declared that this pious object was all they had in view.

Only a small military force was, in fact, dispatched with a body of Jesuits, who established a settlement and began the trade of conversion. Disinterested as this rather expensive expedition appeared, its secret motive might probably be found in the fear that any other nation should establish itself in the neighbourhood of Mexico and the Spanish gold-mines.

The Jesuits came and made converts. These were followed by the Dominicans, who still have settlements, called here missions, in Old California; and subsequently by the Franciscans, who have established themselves in the New. They all convert away at a great rate,—we shall soon find how.

The first missions were seated on the coast of Old California, for the convenience of communication by sea with Mexico, and because the country was favourable to agriculture. The military who accompanied the monks, selected for their residence a situation from whence they could overlook several missions, and be always ready for their defence. These military posts are here called Presidios.

As it was not possible to make the savage natives comprehend the doctrines of Christianity, their inculcation was out of the question; and all that these religionists thought necessary to be done with this simple, timid race, scarcely superior to the animals by whom they were surrounded, was to introduce the Catholic worship, or, more properly, the dominion of the monks, by force of arms. The missions multiplied rapidly. In New California, where we now were, the first of these, that of St. Diego, was established in 1769; now there are twenty-one in this country. Twenty-five thousand baptized Indians belong at present to these missions, and a military force of five hundred dragoons is found sufficient to keep them in obedience, to prevent their escape, or, if they should elude the vigilance of their guards, to bring them from the midst of their numerous tribes, improving the favourable opportunity of making new converts by the power of the sword.

The fate of these so called Christian Indians is not preferable even to that of negro slaves. Abandoned to the despotism of tyrannical monks, Heaven itself offers no refuge from their sufferings; for their spiritual masters stand as porters at the gate, and refuse entrance to whom they please. These unfortunate beings pass their lives in prayer, and in toiling for the monks, without possessing any property of their own. Thrice a day they are driven to church, to hear a mass in the Latin language; the rest of their time is employed in labouring in the fields and gardens with coarse, clumsy implements, and in the evening they are locked up in over-crowded barracks, which, unboarded, and without windows or beds, rather resemble cows' stalls than habitations for men. A coarse woollen shirt which they make themselves, and then receive as a present from the missionaries, constitutes their only clothing. Such is the happiness which the Catholic religion has brought to the uncultivated Indian; and this is the Paradise which he must not presume to undervalue by attempting a return to freedom in the society of his unconverted countrymen, under penalty of imprisonment in fetters.

The large tract of arable land which these pious shepherds of souls have appropriated to themselves, and which is cultivated by their flocks, is for the most part sown with wheat and pulse. The harvest is laid up in store; and what is not necessary for immediate consumption is shipped for Mexico, and there either exchanged for articles required by the missions, or sold for hard piastres to fill the coffers of the monks.

In this way were the missionaries, and the military who depended upon them, living quietly enough in California, when the other Spanish colonies threw off their allegiance to the mother country. The insurrection having spread as far as Mexico, they were invited by the new governments, under advantageous conditions, to make common cause with them, but they remained true to their King; nor was their fidelity shaken by the total neglect of the Spaniards, who for many years appeared to have forgotten their very existence, and had not even troubled themselves to make the ordinary remittances for the pay of the military, or the support of the monks. Still their loyalty remained unshaken; they implicitly obeyed even that command of the King which closed their ports against all foreign vessels; and as the republicans were considered as foreigners, and no ships arrived from Spain, the missions, as well as the Presidios, soon began to suffer the greatest scarcity of many necessaries which the country did not produce. The soldiery, even to the commander himself, were in rags, without pay, and deriving a mendicant subsistence from the monks. The want which pressed most heavily on the latter was that of the implements of agriculture and other labour; having, with true Spanish indolence, forborne any attempt to manufacture them in the country. The very source of all their acquisitions was thus threatened with extinction; yet still they adhered to their King, with a fidelity truly honourable had it been more disinterested:—but what could they expect from a change of government, except the limitations of their hitherto unbounded power?

In the discontent of the soldiers, however, smouldered a spark, dangerous to the power of the monks, which was suddenly blown into a flame by a circumstance that occurred a few years before our arrival.

The only pleasure for which the baptized Indians had ever been indebted to the monks was the possession of such baubles as our sailors use in traffic with the South Sea islanders. These things of course could no longer be obtained, and their loss was regarded by the new Christians as a heavy misfortune. Their despair at length broke out into insurrection: they burst their prisons, and attacked the dwellings of the monks, but retired before the fire of musketry. The military, with very little loss on their side, defeated great numbers of the natives, and brought them again into their previous subjection.

A new light dawned on the minds of the dragoons. What would have become of the monks without their valiant support? Elated by victory, and disregarding all the protestations of the ghostly fathers, whose feebleness and helplessness were now apparent, they declared themselves the first class in the country, and independent of Spain, which for so many years had abandoned them to their fate.

Similar causes produced similar effects in Old California, and each country now forms a separate republic.

Spain might with ease have retained these fertile provinces under allegiance. Had their fidelity received the smallest encouragement, it would probably never have been shaken; and California would have proved a most convenient support for the claims of the mother country on the revolutionized colonies, especially on Mexico, formerly the fertile source of

Spanish wealth. The Philippines have not rebelled, and these rich islands could have afforded all the assistance the missions required. The neglect of California by Spain would almost seem to have been appointed by Providence, that the prosperity of the new States might suffer no interruption.

One immediate result of the independence of this colony is the opening of her ports to all nations, and the consequent impetus given to commerce. The North American States have been the first to make use of the privilege.

The exports of California now consist of corn, ox-hides, tallow, and the costly skins of the sea-otter. Some speculators have attempted a trade with China, but hitherto without success. A richly laden ship was entrusted to a North American captain for this purpose, who disposed of the cargo in China; but found it more convenient to retain both the money and ship for his own use, than to return to the owners.

The government of New California was on our present visit administered by Don Louis Arguello, the same young man with whom I became acquainted on my voyage in the Rurik, when he was commandant of the Presidio of St. Francisco. He resided at this time in Monterey, and employed himself in devising systems of government which should bring the heterogeneous ingredients of the new republic, dragoons, monks, and Indians, into order and unity.

May the destiny of the latter be ameliorated by the change! No Constitution has yet been established here; and Arguello's power, or perhaps ability, was inadequate to introducing that which he had proposed. Many changes are still necessary in the Californias before they can become the happy and flourishing countries for which Nature intended them.

On the morning after our arrival, I visited old Sanchez in the Presidio. He received me with unfeigned cordiality, and related to me many things which had taken place since my visit in the Rurik eight years ago. Don Louis, he said, had become a great man, and he himself a lieutenant, which here imports a considerable rank. Nevertheless, he disapproved of all the proceedings, and felt assured that no good could accrue from them. He would rather, he said, be a petty Spanish subject, than a republican officer of state.

The Presidio was in the same state in which I found it eight years before; and, except the republican flag, no trace of the important changes which had taken place was perceptible. Every thing was going on in the old, easy, careless way.

Sanchez at once promised to provide the ship daily with fresh meat, but advised me to send a boat to the mission of Santa Clara for a supply of vegetables, which were there to be had in superfluity. The Presidio had, with a negligence which would be inconceivable in any other country, omitted to cultivate even sufficient for their own consumption.

As I had not visited the mission of Santa Clara during my first visit to California, I now determined to proceed thither on the following day, in the long-boat. Sanchez provided a good pilot, and sent a courier overland to announce my arrival at the mission.

The bay of St. Francisco is full ninety miles in circuit: it is divided by islands into two pretty equally sized basins, a northern and a southern. On the banks of the southern, which takes an easterly direction, lie the three missions, St. Francisco, Santa Clara, and St. José. Of the northern half of the bay I will speak hereafter.

On the morning of the 28th of September, the Barcasse was ready, and equipped with every thing necessary for our little voyage. Favoured both by wind and tide, we sailed eastward past many charming islands and promontories, to the mission of Santa Clara, which lay at a distance of five-and-twenty miles, in a straight line from the ship. The country presented on all sides a picture of beauty and fertility: the shores are of a moderate elevation, and covered with a brilliant verdure; the hills, towards the interior, swell gently into an amphitheatre, and the background is formed by high thick woods. Groves of oaks are scattered upon the slopes, separated by lovely meadows, and forming more graceful and picturesque groups than I have ever seen as the produce of art. With very little trouble, the most luxuriant harvests might be reaped from this soil; but a happy and industrious population has not yet been established here, to profit from the prodigality of Nature. The death-like stillness of these beautiful fields is broken only by the wild animals which inhabit them; and as far as the eye can reach, it perceives no trace of human existence; not even a canoe is to be seen upon the surrounding waters, which are navigable for large vessels, and boast many excellent harbours;—the large white pelican with the bag under his bill, is the only gainer by the abundance of fish they produce. During the centuries of Spanish supremacy in California, even the exertion of procuring a net has been deemed too great. How abundantly and happily might thousands of families subsist here! and how advantageously might the emigrants to Brazil have preferred this spot for colonization! There, they have to struggle with many difficulties, are often oppressed by the government, and always suffer under a scorching sun. Here, they would have found the climate of the South of Germany, and a luxuriant soil, that would have yielded an ample recompense for the slightest pains bestowed upon it.

After a few hours' sail, we came to a deep creek opening to the right, and on its shores we perceived the mission of St. Francisco rising among wooded hills. The tide by this time had ebbed, the wind had died away, and we proceeded slowly by the aid of oars: this induced us, after rowing about fifteen miles, to land, at noon, on a pleasant little island. We made a blazing fire; and as every sailor understands something of cookery, a dinner was soon dressed, which eaten in the open air in beautiful weather, under the shade of spreading oaks, appeared excellent.

While the sailors were reposing, we examined the island. Its northern shore was tolerably high, and rose almost perpendicularly from the sea. Its soil, as that of all the country about the bay of St. Francisco, consists, under the upper mould, of a variegated slate; probably the foot of man had never before trodden it. But a short time since, no boat was to be found in the neighbourhood, and now each mission possesses only one large barge in which the reverend Fathers pass up and down the rivers that discharge themselves into the northern half of the bay, to seek among the Indians who are occasionally seen on their banks, for proselytes to recruit the ranks of their laborious subjects. The only canoes of the Indians are made of plaited reeds, in which they sit up to their hips in water. That no one has yet attempted to build even the simplest canoe in a country which produces a super-abundance of the finest wood for the purpose, is a striking proof of the indolence of the Spaniards, and the stupidity of the Indians.

Our island was surrounded by wild ducks and other sea-fowl; the white-headed eagle hovered too over the oaks, and seemed to be pursuing a very small species of hare, and a pretty partridge, of which there are great numbers.

We enjoyed for a few hours the recreation of the land, so welcome to sailors, and then continued our voyage with a favourable wind.

The sun was near the horizon when we approached the eastern shore of the bay. Here the water is no longer of sufficient depth to admit large vessels, and the face of the country assumes a different character. The mountains retire to a greater distance; extensive plains slope from the hills towards the water's edge, where they become mere swamps, intersected however by a variety of natural channels, by means of which, boats may run some distance inland. It was already growing dark as we entered these channels, where, even during daylight, the assistance of a good pilot is requisite to thread the intricacies of a navigation among thick reeds that grow to such a height in the marshes on both sides, as to exclude from view every object but the sky. Our sailors plied their oars vigorously; the channels became gradually narrower, and the banks drier; at length we heard human voices behind the reeds, and at midnight we reached the landing-place. A large fire had been lighted. Two dragoons and a few half-naked Indians, sent from the mission, were waiting our arrival, with saddle-horses intended for our use. As the mission was at the distance of a good hour's ride, the night was dark, and I was not inclined to trouble the repose of the monks, I determined to await the dawn of morning. Our small tents were presently pitched, several fires lighted, and the cooks set to work.

After our tedious row, (for, owing to the zigzag course we had been compelled to steer, we had passed over a distance of at least forty miles,) the camping out, in a beautiful night, was quite delightful. Although it was now the latter end of September, the air was as mild as with us during the warmest summer nights. Round our little encampment we heard an incessant barking, as of young dogs, proceeding from a species of wolf, which abounds throughout California; it is not larger than the fox; but is so daring and dexterous, that it makes no scruple of entering human habitations in the night, and rarely fails to appropriate whatever happens to suit it. This we ourselves experienced; for our provision of meat had not been sufficiently secured, and we found nothing in the morning but a gnawed and empty bag.

The rising sun announced the approach of a fine day, and gave us a view of the extensive plains which formed the surrounding country. The missionaries cultivated wheat upon them, which had been already harvested, and large flocks of cattle, horses, and sheep, were seen pasturing among the stubble. The mission of Santa Clara possesses fourteen thousand head of cattle, one thousand horses, and ten thousand sheep. The greater part of these animals being left to roam undisturbed about the woods, they multiply with amazing rapidity.

I now ordered the horses to be saddled, and we set off for the mission, the buildings and woods of which bounded the view over these prodigious corn-fields. Our way lay through the stubble, amongst flocks of wild geese, ducks, and snipes, so tame that we might have killed great numbers with our sticks. These are all birds of passage, spending the winter here, and the summer farther north. We fired a few shots among the geese, and brought down about a dozen: they differ but little in size from our domestic goose, and some of them are quite white. A ride of an hour and a half brought us to Santa Clara, where the monks received us in the most friendly manner, and exerted themselves most hospitably, to make our visit agreeable.

The mission, which was founded in the year 1777, is situated beside a stream of the most pure and delicious water, in a large and extremely fertile plain. The buildings of Santa Clara, overshadowed by thick groves of oaks, and surrounded by gardens which, though carelessly cultivated, produce an abundance of vegetables, the finest grapes, and fruits of all kinds, are in the same style as at all the other missions. They consist of a large stone church, a spacious dwelling-house for the monks, a large magazine for the preservation of corn, and the Rancherios, or barracks, for the Indians, of which mention has already been made. These are divided into long rows of houses, or rather stalls, where each family is allowed a space scarcely large enough to enable them to lie down to repose. We were struck by the appearance of a large quadrangular building, which having no windows on the outside, and only one carefully secured door, resembled a prison for state-criminals. It proved to be the residence appropriated by the monks, the severe guardians of chastity, to the young unmarried Indian women, whom they keep under their particular superintendence, making their time useful to the community by spinning, weaving, and similar occupations. These dungeons are opened two or three times a-day, but only to allow the prisoners to pass to and from the church. I have occasionally seen the poor girls rushing out eagerly to breathe the fresh air, and driven immediately into the church like a flock of sheep, by an old ragged Spaniard armed with a stick. After mass, they are in the same manner hurried back to their prisons. Yet, notwithstanding all the care of the ghostly fathers, the feet of some of these uninviting fair ones were cumbered with bars of iron, the penal consequence, as I was informed, of detected transgression. Only on their marriage are these cloistered virgins allowed to issue from their confinement and associate with their own people in the barracks.

Three times a-day a bell summons the Indians to their meals, which are prepared in large kettles, and served out in portions to each family. They are seldom allowed meat; their ordinary, and not very wholesome food, consisting of wheaten flour, maize, peas and beans, mixed together, and boiled to a thick soup.

The mission of Santa Clara contains fifteen hundred male Indians, of whom about one-half are married. All these men are governed by three monks, and guarded by four soldiers and a subaltern officer. Since this force is found sufficient, it follows either that the Indians of the mission are happier than their free countrymen, or that, no way superior to the domestic animals, they are chained by their instincts to the place where their food is provided. The first supposition can hardly be well founded. Hard labour every day, Sundays only excepted, when labour is superseded by prayer; corporal chastisement, imprisonment, and fetters on the slightest demonstration of disobedience; unwholesome nourishment, miserable lodging, deprivation of all property, and of all the enjoyments of life:— these are not boons which diffuse content. Many indeed of these unfortunate victims prove, by their attempts to escape, that their submission is involuntary; but the soldiers, as I have before observed, generally hunt them from their place of refuge, and bring them back to undergo the severe punishment their transgression has incurred. To the most stupid apathy, then, must the patience of these Indians be ascribed; and in this, their distinguishing characteristic, they exceed every race of men I have ever known, not excepting the degraded natives of Terra del Fuego, or Van Diemen's Land.

The Christian religion, or what the monks are pleased to call by that name, has given no beneficial spur to their minds. How indeed could it act upon their confined understandings, when their teachers were almost wholly deficient in the necessary means of communicating knowledge,—an acquaintance with their language? I have since had opportunities of observing the free Indians, who appear less stupid, and in many respects more civilized, than the proselytes of the *gente rationale*, as the Spaniards here call themselves; and I am convinced that the system of instruction and discipline adopted by the monks, has certainly tended to degrade even these step-children of Nature. If to raise them to the rank of intellectual beings had been really the object in view, rather than making them the mock professors of a religion they are incapable of understanding, they should have been taught the arts of agriculture and architecture, and the method of breeding cattle; they should have been made proprietors of the land they cultivated, and should have freely enjoyed its produce. Had this been done, *los barbaros* might soon have stood on a level with the *gente rationale*.

There are in California many different races of Indians, whose languages vary so much from each other, as sometimes to have scarcely any resemblance; in the single mission of Santa Clara more than twenty languages are spoken. These races are all alike ugly, stupid, dirty, and disgusting: they are of a middle size, weak, and of a blackish colour; they have flat faces, thick lips, broad negro-noses, scarcely any foreheads, and black, coarse, straight hair. The powers of their mind lie yet profoundly dormant; and La Pérouse does not perhaps exaggerate when he affirms, that if any one among them can be made to comprehend that twice two make four, he may pass, in comparison with his countrymen, for a Descartes or a Newton. To most of them, this important arithmetical proposition would certainly be perfectly incomprehensible.

In their wild state, all these Indians lead a wandering life. It is only recently that they have begun to build huts of underwood, which they burn whenever they remove from the spot. The chase is their sole occupation and means of subsistence. Hence their skill in shooting with arrows has cost many Spanish lives. They lie in wait at night, in the forests and mountains, watching for game.

Agriculture, as I have before observed, is the copious source of revenue to the monks, and they farm on an extensive scale. The yearly crop of wheat at Santa Clara alone, produces three thousand fanegos, about six hundred and twenty English quarters, or three thousand four hundred Berlin bushels; and from the extraordinary fertility of the soil, the harvest, on an average, is forty-fold, notwithstanding the roughness of their mode of cultivation. The field is first broken up with a very clumsy plough, then sown, and a second ploughing completes the work. Under the hard clods of earth thus left undisturbed, a great part of the seed perishes of course. How unexampled would be the harvest, if assisted by the capital and industry of an European farmer!

The monks themselves confess that they are not good agriculturists; but they are content with their harvests. Their carelessness is however unpardonable, in having never yet erected a mill. There is not one in all California; and the poor Indians are obliged to grind their corn by manual labour between two large, flat stones.

From the mission we took half an hour's walk to a *Pueblo*. This word signifies, in California, a village, inhabited by married invalids, disbanded soldiers from the Presidio, and their progeny. This Pueblo lies in a beautiful spot. The houses are pleasant, built of stone, and stand in the midst of orchards, and hedges of vines bearing luxuriant clusters of the richest grapes. The inhabitants came out to meet us, and with much courteousness, blended with the ceremonious politeness of the Spaniards, invited us to enter their simple but cleanly dwellings. All their countenances bespoke health and contentment, and they have good cause to rejoice in their lot. Unburthened by taxes of any kind, and in possession of as much land as they choose to cultivate, they live free from care on the rich produce of their fields and herds.

The population of these Pueblos is every year on the increase; while, on the contrary, the numbers of the Indians dependent on the missions are continually decreasing. The mortality amongst the latter is so great, that the establishments could not continue, if their spiritual conductors did not constantly procure fresh recruits from amongst the free Indians, to fill the thinning ranks of their labourers.

In Old California, many of the missions have gone to decay on account of the total extermination of the savages. The north still affords an abundant supply to New California; but if the missionaries do not economize the lives of their men more than they have hitherto done, this source also will in time be exhausted. Meanwhile the Pueblos will continue to multiply, and will become the origins of a new and improved population.

After passing three days with the monks of Santa Clara, who at least possess the virtue of hospitality, we set out on our return with a provision of fruit and vegetables, purchased for very fair prices. They were carried to the place of embarkation on heavy and very badly constructed cars drawn by oxen: the wheels were made of thick planks nailed together, without any regard to mechanical science either in their form or poizing; and the machine slowly advanced with a difficult jolting motion very prejudicial to our fine melons, peaches, grapes, and figs, and to the magnificent apples, which have no equals in Europe. On reaching our Barcasse, we found all in readiness to receive ourselves and cargo. The sailors had been much disturbed in the night by the wolves.

The ebb-tide favoured our navigation, and soon brought us within sight of an arm of the sea, stretching eastward, at the extremity of which the mission of St. José was built in the year 1797, on a very fertile spot. It is already one of the richest in California, and a Pueblo has arisen in its neighbourhood; the only Pueblo on the Bay of St. Francisco, except that near Santa Clara. Between St. José and Santa Clara a road has lately been made which may be traversed on horseback in about two hours.

Soon after our return to the ship, a monk was observed riding along the shore in company with a dragoon, and making signs with his large hat, that he wished to come on board. We sent the boat for him, and a little, thin, lively, and loquacious Spaniard introduced himself as the Padre Thomas of the mission of St. Francisco, and offered, for a good remuneration, to furnish us daily with fresh provisions, besides two bottles of milk. He boasted not a little of being the only man in the whole Bay of St. Francisco who had succeeded, after overcoming many difficulties and obstacles, in obtaining milk from cows, of which he had a numerous herd. As the Presidio could not supply our wants, and the mission of Santa Clara lay too far off, we were very willing to accede to Padre Thomas's wish; and he left us with an invitation to visit him the following noon.

Accordingly, several of my officers and myself rode the next day to the mission of St. Francisco, which I have described in the account of my former voyage, and which has remained pretty much in the same state ever since. The jovial Father Thomas was now the only monk in the mission, and, consequently, at its head; he entertained us in a very friendly manner, and with considerable expense.

The repast consisted of a great number of dishes, strongly seasoned with garlic and pepper, and plenty of very tolerable wine of the Padre's own vintage; it was animated by music, partly the performance of some little naked Indian boys, upon bad fiddles, and partly of the venerable father himself on a barrel organ which stood near him. The fruits for the dessert were procured from the mission of Santa Clara, as the mists from the sea prevent their ripening at St. Francisco.

Some guns from the Presidio, fired with the powder that remained after returning our salute, one morning announced the arrival of Don Ignatio Martinez, the commandant, who, after the breaking up of the congress at Monterey, had returned to his post. With him came also the commandant of the Presidio St. Diego, Don José Maria Estudillo, whom I had before known. They visited me, accompanied by Sanchez, dined with me on board, and were so well entertained, that they did not take leave of us till late at night.

Indispensable business now summoned me to the establishment of the Russian-American Company called Ross, which lies about eighty miles north of St. Francisco. I had for some time been desirous of performing the journey by land, but the difficulties had appeared insurmountable. Without the assistance of the commandant, it certainly could not have been accomplished; I was therefore glad to avail myself of his friendly disposition towards me to make the attempt. We required a number of horses and a military escort; the latter to serve us at once as guides, and as a protection against the savages. Both these requests were immediately granted; and Don Estudillo himself offered to command our escort.

My companions on this journey were Dr. Eschscholz, Mr. Hoffman, two of my officers, two sailors, Don Estudillo, and four dragoons, making altogether a party of twelve. On the evening previous to the day for our departure, Estudillo came to the ship with his four dragoons, the latter well armed, and accoutred in a panoply of leather. He himself, in the old Spanish costume, with a heavy sword, still heavier spurs, a dagger and pistols in his belt, and a staff in his hand, was a good personification of an adventurer of the olden time. He assured us that we could not be too cautious, since we should pass through a part of the country inhabited by "*los Indianos bravos.*" we therefore also made a plentiful provision of arms, and were ready, as soon as the first beams of morning glimmered on the tops of the mountains, to set forward in our barcasse for the mission of St. Gabriel, lying on the northern shore of the bay, whence our land journey was to commence.

The weather was beautiful, the wind perfectly still, and the air enchantingly mild. An Indian named Marco, whom Estudillo had brought with him, served us as pilot; for the Spaniards here, incapable, either through indolence or ignorance, of discharging that office, always employ an experienced Indian at the helm.

Don Estudillo, although advanced in life, was a very cheerful companion, and one of the most enlightened Spaniards I have met with in California. He piqued himself a little on his literary acquirements, and mentioned having read three books besides Don Quixote and Gil Blas, whilst, as he assured me in confidence, the rest of his countrymen here had hardly ever seen any other book than the Bible. Marco had grown grey in the mission: on account of his usefulness, he had been in many respects better treated than most of the Indians: he spoke Spanish with tolerable fluency; and when Estudillo endeavoured to exercise his wit upon him, often embarrassed him not a little by his repartees. This Marco affords a proof that, under favourable circumstances, the minds even of the Indians of California are susceptible of improvement; but these examples are rare in the missions.

Don Estudillo spoke with much freedom of the affairs of California, where he had resided thirty years: like most of his comrades, he was no friend to the clergy. He accused them of consulting only their own interest, and of employing their proselytes as a means of laying up wealth for themselves, with which, when acquired, they return to Spain. He described to us their method of conversion. The monks, he said, send dragoons into the mountains to catch the free heathens, that they may convert them into Christian slaves. For this species of chase, the huntsman is provided with a strong leathern noose fastened to his saddle, long enough to throw to a great distance, and acquires such dexterity in the practice as seldom to miss his aim. As soon as he perceives a troop of Indians, he throws his noose over one of them before he has time to defend himself, then setting spurs to his horse, rides back to the mission with his prisoner, and is fortunate if he bring him there alive. I can myself bear witness to the skill and boldness of the dragoons, in the management of their horses, and in the use of the noose, with which two or three of them in conjunction will catch even bears and wild bulls; a single man is sufficient to capture an Indian.

Estudillo declared that no Indian ever presents himself voluntarily at the missions, but that they are all either hunted in the manner above described, or tricked out of their liberty by some artifice of the monks. For this purpose, some few in every mission are extremely well treated, as for instance our pilot Marco. These are from time to time sent into distant parts of the country to exert their eloquence on their countrymen, and entice them to the missions. Once there, they are immediately baptized, and they then become for ever the property of the monks.

To my observation, that affairs would now probably assume a different aspect, as the arbitrary dominion of the clergy, and the dependence of the military upon them were equally terminated, Estudillo replied, that California might certainly become a powerful state,—that she was abundantly provided by nature with all that was requisite to her political aggrandizement, but that she needed a man of ability in her councils. "Don Louis Arguello," said he, "is not the man to re-invigorate our radically disordered finances, to introduce a wholesome subordination, without which no government can flourish, and to establish a constitution upon which our future tranquillity and improvement may be founded. Our soldiers are all of one mind; whoever pays them the arrears due from the Spanish government is their master; he purchases them, and to him they belong. Induced by a knowledge of this disposition, Mexico has entered into negotiations with us; and the question whether California shall exist as an independent state, or place herself under the protection of another power, has been particularly discussed at the late congress at Monterey, and is still undecided."

I confess I could not help speculating upon the benefit this country would derive from becoming a province of our powerful empire, and how useful it would prove to Russia. An inexhaustible granary for Kamtschatka, Ochotsk, and all the settlements of the American Company; these regions, so often afflicted with a scarcity of corn, would derive new life from a close connection with California.

The sun rose in full magnificence from behind the mountain, at the moment when, emerging from between the islands which divide the northern from the southern half of the bay, an extensive mirror of water opened upon our view. The mission of St. Gabriel, the first stage of our journey, formed a distinguished object in the background of the prospect, sloping up the sides of the hills, the intervening flat land lying so low that it was not yet within our horizon. We had also a distant view towards the north-west of another newly founded mission, that of St. Francisco Salona, the only one situated on the northern shore of the bay except St. Gabriel.

The country at this side of the bay, chiefly characterised by gently swelling hills, the park-like grouping of the trees, and the lively verdure of the meadows, is as agreeable to the eye as that of the southern coast. The water is pure and wholesome, which that at the Presidio is not; we therefore laid in our ship's store here.

The whole Bay of St. Francisco, in which thousands of ships might lie at anchor, is formed by nature for an excellent harbour; but the little creeks about the north-west coast, now lying to our left, and which I have since frequently visited, are especially advantageous for repairs, being so deep that the largest vessels can lie conveniently close to the land; and an abundance of the finest wood for ship-building, even for the tallest masts, is found in the immediate neighbourhood. The whole of the northern part of the bay, which does not properly belong to California, but is assigned by geographers to New Albion, has hitherto remained unvisited by voyagers, and little known even to the Spaniards residing in the country. Two large navigable rivers, which I afterwards surveyed, empty themselves into it, one from the north, the other from the east. The land is extremely fruitful, and the climate is perhaps the finest and most healthy in the world. It has hitherto been the fate of these regions, like that of modest merit or humble virtue, to remain unnoticed; but posterity will do them justice; towns and cities will hereafter flourish where all is now desert; the waters, over which scarcely a solitary boat is yet seen to glide, will reflect the flags of all nations; and a happy, prosperous people receiving with thankfulness what prodigal Nature bestows for their use, will disperse her treasures over every part of the world.

A fresh and favourable wind brought us, without much delay from the opposing ebb-tide, to the northern shore. We left the common embouchure of its two principal rivers, distinguished by the steepness of their banks to the right, and rowing up the narrow channel which has formed itself through the marsh land, reached our landing-place just as the sun's disk touched the blue summits of the mountains in the west.

We were still distant a good nautical mile from the mission of St. Gabriel, which peeped from amongst the foliage of its ancient oaks. Many horses belonging to the mission were grazing on a beautiful meadow by the water-side, in perfect harmony with a herd of small deer, which are very numerous in this country. Our dragoons, who had no inclination for a long walk, took their *lassos* in hand, and soon caught us as many horses as we wanted. We had brought our saddles with us, and a delightful gallop across the plain carried us to St. Gabriel, where we were received in a very hospitable manner by the only monk in residence.

The locality of this mission, founded in 1816, is still better chosen than that of the celebrated Santa Clara. A mountain shelters it from the injurious north-wind; but the same mountain serves also as a hiding-place and bulwark for the *Indianos bravos*, who have already once succeeded in burning the buildings of the mission, and still keep the monks continually on the watch against similar depredations. In fact, St. Gabriel has quite the appearance of an outpost for the defence of the other missions.

The garrison, *six men* strong, is always ready for service on the slightest alarm. Having been driven from my bed at night by the vermin, I saw two sentinels, fully armed, keeping guard towards the mountain, each of them beside a large fire; every two minutes they rang a bell which was hung between two pillars, and were regularly answered by the howling of the little wolf I have before spoken of, as often lurking in the vicinity of the missions. That there is not much to fear from other enemies, is sufficiently proved by the small number of soldiers kept, and the total neglect of all regular means of defence. The courage of these *bravos* seems indeed principally to consist in unwillingness to be caught, in flying with all speed to their hiding-places when pursued, and in setting fire to any property of the missions when they can find an opportunity of doing so unobserved. We saw here several of these heroes working patiently enough with irons on their feet, and in no way distinguishable in manners or appearance from their brethren of St. Francisco or Santa Clara.

With the first rays of the sun we mounted our horses, and having passed the valley of St. Gabriel, and the hill which bounds it, our guide led us in a north-westerly direction further into the interior. The fine, light, and fertile soil we rode upon was thickly covered with rich herbage, and the luxuriant trees stood in groups as picturesque as if they had been disposed by the hand of taste. We met with numerous herds of small stags, so fearless, that they suffered us to ride fairly into the midst of them, but then indeed darted away with the swiftness of an arrow. We sometimes also, but less frequently, saw another species of stag, as large as a horse, with branching antlers; these generally graze on hills, from whence they can see round them on all sides, and appear much more cautious than the small ones. The Indians, however, have their contrivances to take them. They fasten a pair of the stag's antlers on their heads, and cover their bodies with his skin; then crawling on all-fours among the high grass, they imitate the movements of the creature while grazing; the herd, mistaking them for their fellows, suffer them to approach without suspicion, and are not aware of the treachery till the arrows of the disguised foes have thinned their number.

Towards noon the heat became so oppressive, that we were obliged to halt on the summit of a hill: we reposed under the shade of some thick and spreading oaks, while our horses grazed and our meal was preparing. During our rest, we caught a glimpse of a troop of Indians skulking behind some bushes at a distance; our dragoons immediately seized their arms, but the savages disappeared without attempting to approach us. In a few hours we proceeded on our journey, through a country, which presenting no remarkable object to direct our course, excited my astonishment at the local memory of our guide, who had traversed it but once before. Two great shaggy white wolves, hunting a herd of small deer, fled in terror on our appearance, and we had the gratification of saving the pretty animals for this time. In several places we saw little cylindrically-shaped huts of underwood, which appeared to have been recently quitted by Indians, and sometimes we even found the still glimmering embers of a fire; it is therefore probable that the savages were often close to us when we were not aware of it; but they always took care to conceal themselves from the much dreaded dragoons and their lassos.

In the evening we reached a little mountain brook, which, after winding through a ravine, falls into the sea at Port Romanzow, or Bodega. It was already dark, and though but ten miles distance from Ross, we were obliged to pass the chill and foggy night not very agreeably on this spot. In the morning we forded the shallow stream, and as we proceeded, found in the bold, wild features of the scene a striking difference from the smiling valleys through which we had travelled on the preceding day. The nearer we drew to the coast, the more abrupt became the precipices and the higher the rocks, which were overgrown with larch even to their peaked summits.

We wound round the bases of some hills, and having with much fatigue climbed other very steep ascents, reached towards noon a considerable height, which rewarded us with a magnificent prospect. Amongst the remarkable objects before us, the ocean stretched to the west, with the harbour of Romanzow, which unfortunately will only afford admission to small vessels; the Russian settlement here, can therefore never be as prosperous as it might have been, had circumstances permitted its establishment on the bay of St. Francisco. To the east, extending far inland, lay a valley, called by the Indians the Valley of the White Men. There is a tradition among them, that a ship was once wrecked on this coast; that the white men chose this valley for their residence, and lived there in great harmony with the Indians. What afterwards became of them is not recorded. On the north-east was a high mountain thickly covered with fir trees, from amongst which rose dark columns of smoke, giving evidence of Indian habitations. Our soldiers said that it was the abode of a chief and his tribe, whose valour had won the respect of the Spaniards; that they were of a distinct class from the common race of Indians; had fixed their dwellings on this mountain on account of its supposed inaccessibility; were distinguished for their courage, and preferred death to the dominion of the Missionaries, into whose power no one of them has ever yet been entrapped. Is it not possible that they may owe their superiority to having mingled their race with that of the shipwrecked whites?

Our road now lay sometimes across hills and meadows, and sometimes along the sands so near the ocean that we were sprinkled by its spray. We passed Port Romanzow, and soon after forded the bed of another shallow river to which the Russians have given the name of Slavianka. Farther inland it is said to be deeper, and even navigable for ships; its banks are extremely fertile, but peopled by numerous warlike hordes. It flows hither from the north-east; and the Russians have proceeded up it a distance of a hundred wersts, or about sixty-seven English miles.

The region we now passed through was of a very romantic though wild character; and the luxuriant growth of the grass proved that the soil was rich. From the summit of a high hill, we at length, to our great joy, perceived beneath us the fortress of Ross, to which we descended by a tolerably convenient road. We spurred our tired horses, and excited no small astonishment as we passed through the gate at a gallop. M. Von

Schmidt, the governor of the establishment, received us in the kindest manner, fired some guns to greet our arrival on Russian-American ground, and conducted us into his commodious and orderly mansion, built in the European fashion with thick beams.

The settlement of Ross, situated on the sea-shore, in latitude 38° 33', and on an insignificant stream, was founded in the year 1812, with the free consent of the natives, who were very useful in furnishing materials for the buildings and even in their erection.

The intention in forming this settlement was to pursue the chase of the sea-otter on the coast of California, where the animal was then numerous, as it had become extremely scarce in the more northern establishments. The Spaniards who did not hunt them, willingly took a small compensation for their acquiescence in the views of the Russians; and the sea-otter, though at present scarce even here, is more frequently caught along the Californian coast, southward from Ross, than in any other quarter. The fortress is a quadrangle, palisaded with tall, thick beams, and defended by two towers which mount fifteen cannons. The garrison consisted, on my arrival, of a hundred and thirty men, of whom a small number only were Russians, the rest Aleutians.

The Spaniards lived at first on the best terms with the new settlers, and provided them with oxen, cows, horses, and sheep; but when in process of time they began to remark that, notwithstanding the inferiority of soil and climate, the Russian establishment became more flourishing than theirs, envy, and apprehension of future danger, took possession of their minds: they then required that the settlement should be abandoned,—asserted that their rights of dominion extended northward quite to the Icy Sea, and threatened to support their claims by force of arms.

The founder and then commander of the fortress of Ross, a man of penetration, and one not easily frightened, gave a very decided answer. He had, he said, at the command of his superiors, settled in this region, which had not previously been in the possession of any other power, and over which, consequently, none had a right but the natives; that these latter had freely consented to his occupation of the land, and therefore that he would yield to no such unfounded pretension as that now advanced by the Spaniards, but should be always ready to resist force by force.

Perceiving that the Russians would not comply with their absurd requisitions, and considering that they were likely to be worsted in an appeal to arms, the Spaniards quietly gave up all further thought of hostilities, and entered again into friendly communications with our people; since which the greatest unity has subsisted between the two nations. The Spaniards often find Ross very serviceable to them. For instance, there is no such thing as a smith in all California; consequently the making and repairing of all manner of iron implements here is a great accommodation to them, and affords lucrative employment to the Russians. The dragoons who accompanied us, had brought a number of old gunlocks to be repaired.

In order that the Russians might not extend their dominion to the northern shore of the Bay of St. Francisco, the Spaniards immediately founded the missions of St. Gabriel and St. Francisco Salona. It is a great pity that we were not beforehand with them. The advantages of possessing this beautiful bay are incalculable, especially as we have no harbour but the bad one of Bodega or Port Romanzow.

The inhabitants of Ross live in the greatest concord with the Indians, who repair, in considerable numbers, to the fortress, and work as day-labourers, for wages. At night they usually remain outside the palisades. They willingly give their daughters in marriage to Russians and Aleutians; and from these unions ties of relationship have arisen which strengthen the good understanding between them. The inhabitants of Ross have often penetrated singly far into the interior, when engaged in the pursuit of deer or other game, and have passed whole nights among different Indian tribes, without ever having experienced any inconvenience. This the Spaniards dare not venture upon. The more striking the contrast between the two nations in their treatment of the savages, the more ardently must every friend to humanity rejoice on entering the Russian territory.

The Greek Church does not make converts by force. Free from fanaticism, she preaches only toleration and love. She does not even admit of persuasion, but trusts wholly to conviction for proselytes, who, when once they enter her communion, will always find her a loving mother. How different has been the conduct both of Catholic priests and Protestant missionaries!

The climate at Ross is mild. Reaumur's thermometer seldom falls to the freezing point; yet gardens cannot flourish, on account of the frequent fogs. Some wersts farther inland, beyond the injurious influence of the fog, plants of the warmest climates prosper surprisingly. Cucumbers of fifty pounds' weight, gourds of sixty-five, and other fruits in proportion, are produced in them. Potatoes yield a hundred or two hundred fold, and, as they will produce two crops in a year, are an effectual security against famine. The fortress is surrounded by wheat and barley fields, which, on account of the fogs, are less productive than those of Santa Clara, but which still supply sufficient corn for the inhabitants of Ross. The Aleutians find their abode here so agreeable, that although very unwilling to leave their islands, they are seldom inclined to return to them.

The Spaniards should take a lesson in husbandry from M. Von Schmidt, who has brought it to an admirable degree of perfection. Implements, equal to the best we have in Europe, are made here under his direction. Our Spanish companions were struck with admiration at what he had done; but what astonished them most, was the effect of a windmill; they had never before seen a machine so ingenious, and so well adapted to its purpose.

Ross is blest with an abundance of the finest wood for building. The sea provides it with the most delicious fish, the land with an inexhaustible quantity of the best kinds of game; and, notwithstanding the want of a good harbour, the northern settlements might easily find in this a plentiful magazine for the supply of all their wants. Two ships had already run in here from Stapel.

The Indians of Ross are so much like those of the missions, that they may well be supposed to belong to the same race, however different their language. They appear indeed by no means so stupid, and are much more cheerful and contented than at the missions, where a deep melancholy always clouds their faces, and their eyes are constantly fixed upon the ground; but this difference is only the natural result of the different treatment they experience. They have no permanent residence, but wander about naked, and, when not employed by the Russians as day-labourers, follow no occupation but the chase. They are not difficult in the choice of their food, but consume the most disgusting things, not excepting all kinds of worms and insects, with good appetite, only avoiding poisonous snakes. For the winter they lay up a provision of acorns and wild rye: the latter grows here very abundantly. When it is ripe, they burn the straw away from it, and thus roast the corn, which is then raked together, mixed with acorns, and eaten without any farther preparation. The Indians here have invented several games of chance: they are passionately fond of gaming, and often play away every thing they possess. Should the blessing of civilization ever be extended to the rude inhabitants of these regions, the merit will be due to the Russian settlements, certainly not to the Spanish missions.

After a stay of two days, we took leave of the estimable M. Von Schmidt, and returned by the same way that we came, without meeting with any remarkable occurrence. Professor Eschscholtz remained at Ross, in order to prosecute some botanical researches, intending to rejoin us by means of an Aleutian baidar, several of which were shortly to proceed to St. Francisco in search of otters. This promised chase was a gratifying circumstance to me, as I had it in contemplation to examine several of the rivers that fall into the Bay of St. Francisco, for which purpose the small Aleutian vessels would probably prove extremely serviceable. The northwest wind is prevalent here during summer, and rain is unknown in that season: it was now, however, the latter end of October, and southerly gales began to blow, accompanied by frequent showers; we had therefore to wait some time for the baidars and Professor Eschscholtz. Meanwhile, to our great surprise, a boat with six oars, one day, entered the bay from the open sea, and lay to beside our ship. It belonged to an English whaler, which had been tacking about for some days, and was prevented by the contrary wind from getting into the bay. The greater part of his crew being sick of the scurvy, the captain at length resolved on sending his boat ashore, in hopes of being able to get some fresh provisions for his patients. I immediately furnished the boat with an ample supply both of fresh meat and vegetables, and having completed its little cargo, it proceeded again to sea forthwith. The next day the whaler succeeded in getting into the bay, and came to anchor close alongside. It was evident, from their manner of working the vessel, that she had but few hands on board capable of labour. The captain, who shortly afterwards visited me, was himself suffering severely, and his mates were all confined to their beds; seven months the vessel had been at sea off the Japanese coast, holding no communication with the shore; and this without having succeeded in the capture of a single whale, though numbers of them had been seen on the coast. The scurvy with which the crew was afflicted, was mainly attributable to unwholesome food, selected on a principle of unpardonable economy, and to the want of cleanliness; a vice not usual among the English, but which, during so long an absence from land, is scarcely to be avoided; not the slightest symptom of this fearful malady, formerly so fatal to seamen, manifested itself on board my vessel throughout the whole course of our tedious voyage.

The captain informed me that a number of whalers frequented the Japanese coast, and often obtained rich cargoes in a short period: the principal disadvantages with which they had to contend were violent storms, and a strict prohibition against landing. The Japanese, as is well known, refuse to have any foreign intercourse except with the Chinese and Dutch, and treat all other nations as if they carried contagion with them; hoping thus to preserve their ancient manners unchanged. During my first voyage with Admiral Krusenstern, I spent seven months in Japan, and may venture to assert, that whoever has an opportunity of becoming acquainted with the people, cannot but respect them for the high degree of intellectual development to which they have attained, through their own efforts, unassisted by foreign influence. Their total isolation is probably owing to the timid policy of a despotic government, anxious to prevent the introduction of ideas that might possibly exercise a hostile influence upon the existing institutions.

A whaler that had exceeded his appointed stay on the coast, had completely exhausted his stock of water and provisions. In this distress, although fully aware of the severe prohibition, the captain resolved to pay a visit to the Emperor in his capital, and accordingly, without ceremony, sailed into the Bay of Jeddo, where he cast anchor within gun-shot of the city. The hubbub among the inhabitants, who had never seen an European vessel before, may be imagined. The shore immediately swarmed with soldiers, and armed boats surrounded the ship. From these martial preparations, the crew apprehended that it was intended to make them pay for their temerity with their lives; but their fears proved unfounded. As soon as the Japanese had taken the necessary precautions to prevent the vessel either from leaving the spot where she had first anchored, or from sending a boat on shore, a handsome barge came alongside, from which two Bonjoses, dressed in silk, and each armed with two sabres, stepped on board: they were accompanied by an interpreter who spoke a little broken Dutch. They saluted the captain politely, inquiring the object of his visit, and whether he was not aware that the coast of Japan was not accessible under pain of death? The captain acknowledged himself aware of the prohibition, but stated that the emergency of the case had left him no choice: the Bonjoses thereupon searched the vessel, and having satisfied themselves that she was really destitute of provisions and water, they took leave of the captain with the same civility they had shown him on their arrival. A multitude of boats with persons of both sexes now issued from the city, to feast their eyes upon the novel spectacle, but they were not allowed to approach within the circle marked by the watch-boats. The same day, the interpreter returned, bringing water and every species of provisions, sufficient for several weeks, declaring that the Emperor furnished every thing gratuitously, as the government would deem it a disgrace to accept payment from those whom distress had driven to their shore; but as the captain's necessities were now provided for, he was ordered immediately to put to sea, and to inform his countrymen, that except in cases of the most urgent necessity, they were not permitted to approach the Japanese coast under pain of death; nor was it at all just to carry on a fishery on their coast, without the permission of the Emperor. The interpreter had brought a number of people with him, who assisted in shipping the provisions and water: the captain was then immediately obliged to weigh anchor, and the Japanese boats towed the vessel out to sea, after she had been scarcely twelve hours in the bay. On taking leave, the captain wished to make a present to the interpreter, but he hastened out of the vessel in alarm, declaring that his acceptance of the smallest trifle would cost him his head. Europeans are not so scrupulous.

Soon after this, another whaler, knowing nothing about the affair in Jeddo, sent a boat ashore, a hundred miles farther south, to a little village on the coast, to try and purchase some fresh provisions. The sailors, on landing, were immediately seized and imprisoned, and their boat placed under arrest. The ship, having waited a long time in vain for the return of her boat, was at length driven by a violent storm to a distance from the coast. The prisoners were well treated; their prison was commodious, and their food excellent. In fourteen days, sentence was pronounced on them, probably at Jeddo, and proved less mild than might have been expected in Japan:—they were ordered to be replaced in their boat, and immediately sent to sea without any provisions, let the weather be what it might. After wandering on the trackless ocean for eight-and-forty hours, they had the good fortune to meet with a whaler, which took them in. These examples may serve as a warning to all navigators who may be desirous of effecting a landing in Japan.

The Californian winter being now fairly set in, we had much rain and frequent storms. On the 9th of October the south-west wind blew with the violence of the West-Indian tornado, rooted up the strongest trees, tore off the roofs of the houses, and occasioned great devastation in the cultivated lands. One of our thickest cables broke; and if the second had given way, we would have been driven on the rocky shore of the channel which unites the bay with the sea, where a powerful current struggling with the tempest produced a frightful surf. Fortunately, the extreme violence of the storm lasted only a few hours, but in that short time it caused a destructive inundation: the water spread so rapidly over the low lands, that our people had scarcely time to secure the tent, with the astronomical apparatus. On comparing the time of day at St. Petersburg and St. Francisco, by means of the difference of longitude, it appears that the tremendous inundation at the former city took place not only on the same day, but even began in the same hour as that in California. Several hundred miles westward, on the Sandwich Islands, the wind raged with similar fury at the same time, as it did also still farther off, upon the Philippine Islands, where it was accompanied by an earthquake. So violent was the storm in the Bay of Manilla, (usually so safe a harbour,) that a French corvette, at anchor there, under the command of Captain Bougainville, a son of the celebrated navigator, was entirely dismasted, as we afterwards heard, on the Sandwich Islands, and at Manilla itself. This hurricane, therefore, raged at the same time over the greatest part of the northern hemisphere; the causes which produced it may possibly have originated beyond our atmosphere.

Finding that our anchorage would not be secure during the winter, if we should be exposed to storms of this kind, we took advantage of the fine weather on the following day, to sail some miles farther eastward, into a little bay surrounded by a romantic landscape, where Vancouver formerly lay, and which is perfectly safe at all seasons: the Spaniards have named this bay *Herba buena*, after a sweet-smelling herb which grows on its shores.

The arrival of Dr. Eschscholtz and the baidars from Ross was still delayed, and I really began to fear that some misfortune had befallen them in the tempest: my joy therefore was extreme, when at last, on the 12th of October, the baidars, twenty in number, entered the harbour undamaged, and we received our friend again safe and well. The little flotilla had indeed left Ross before the commencement of the hurricane, but had fortunately escaped any injury from it, by taking refuge at a place called *Cap de los Reges*, till its fury was expended; but the voyagers had been obliged to bivouack on the naked rock, without shelter from the weather, and with very scanty provisions. Dr. Eschscholtz, however, not in the slightest degree disheartened by the difficulties he had undergone, was quite ready to join the voyage I had meditated for the examination of the adjacent rivers.

All our preparations were now completed; we again took on board our pilot Marco, and a soldier from the Presidio, who offered to accompany us. On the 18th of November the weather was favourable, and we set out with a barcasse and a shallop, both well manned and provided with every necessary, in company with the Aleutian flotilla. At first we took the same course I have before described, towards the mission of St. Gabriel; cutting through the waters of the southern basin, and working our way between the islands into the northern portion of the bay; then adopting an easterly course, so that St. Gabriel remained at a considerable distance to the left in the north-east. We reached towards noon, at a distance of thirty miles from our ship, the common mouth of the two before-mentioned rivers, which here fall into the bay.

The breadth of this embouchure is a mile and a half, and the banks on both sides are high, steep, and little wooded. It is crossed by a shallow, not above two or three feet deep; but on its east side the channel will admit ships of a middling size fully laden. The current was so strong against us, that it was with much exertion our rowers accomplished crossing the shallow. We landed on the left bank in order to determine the geographical position of the mouth, and found the latitude 38° 2' 4", and the longitude 122° 4'. After finishing this task, I ascended the highest hillock on the shore, which consisted of strata of slate and quartz, to admire the beauty of the prospect. On the south lay the enviable and important Bay of St. Francisco with its many islands and creeks; to the north flowed the broad beautiful river formed by the junction of the two, sometimes winding between high, steep rocks, sometimes gliding among smiling meadows, where numerous herds of deer were grazing. In every direction the landscape was charming and luxuriant. Our Aleutians here straggled about in their little baidars, and pursued the game with which land and water were stocked: they had never seen it in such plenty; and being passionately fond of the chase, they fired away without ceasing, and even brought down some of the game with a javelin. The Aleutians are as much at home in their little leathern canoes, as our Cossacks on horseback. They follow their prey with the greatest rapidity in all directions, and it seldom escapes them. White and grey pelicans about twice the size of our geese were here in great numbers. An Aleutian followed a flock of these birds, and killed one of them with his javelin; the rest of the flock took this so ill, that they attacked the murderer and beat him severely with their wings, before other baidars could come to his assistance. The frequent appearance of the pelican on this river, proves that it abounds in fish; a remark that our pilot Marco confirmed; and we ourselves saw many large fish leap to the surface of the water.

When the sailors had rested some hours, we continued our voyage up the stream; but it was ebb-tide, and both currents united allowed us to make but little progress. We landed therefore at six o'clock, after working only a few miles, and pitched our tents for the night in a pretty meadow. The river flowing as before, from the north, was here a mile broad, and deep enough for the largest ships.

On the following morning we broke up our camp at break of day, and, favoured by wind and tide, sailed swiftly forward in a direction almost due north. The aspect of the river now frequently changed: its breadth varied from one to two and three miles. We often came into large reaches many miles in circumference, and surrounded by magnificent scenery. We sailed past pretty hilly islands adorned with lofty spreading trees, and every where found a sufficient depth of water to admit the largest ships. The steep banks sometimes opened to delightful plains, where the deer were grazing under the shadow of luxuriant oaks. The voyage was in fact, even at this time of year, a most agreeable excursion.

When we had proceeded eighteen miles from our night camp, and twenty-three from the river's mouth, we reached the confluence of the two streams. One flows from the east, and the other from the north. The Spaniards call the first Pescadores; farther inland it receives two other rivers, which, according to our pilot, are equally broad and deep as itself: the missionaries have given them the names of St. Joachim, and Jesus Maria. Some way up these rivers, whose banks are said to have been uncommonly fertile and thickly peopled, the pious fathers have journeyed to convert the Indians and procure labourers for the missions. Now that a part of the natives have yielded to conversion, and others have fled farther into the interior to escape it, no human being is to be found in the tract of land which we were surveying; no trace remains of a numerous race called Korekines, by whom it was once inhabited. Since the river Pescadores was already known, I chose the other, which flows from the north, and is called Sacramento. Towards noon, after we had ascended it some miles, a violent contrary wind forced us ashore; latitude 38° 22'.

The wind increasing every moment in strength, we were obliged to give up for this day all thoughts of making farther progress; and resolving to pass the night here, pitched our tents in a pleasant meadow on the west side of the river. I then climbed a hill, to enjoy a more extensive prospect; and observed that the country to the west swelled into hills of a moderate height, besprinkled with trees growing singly. In the east and south-east the horizon was bounded by icy mountains, the Sierra Nevada, part of the immense chain which divides America from north to south: they appeared to be covered more than half-way down with ice and snow. The distance of these mountains from my present station could not be less than forty miles. Between them and the river the country is low, flat, thickly wooded, and crossed by an infinite number of streams, which divide the whole of it into islands. We had not yet met a single Indian; but the columns of smoke which rose from this abundantly irrigated tract of land, showed that they had taken refuge where the dragoons and their lassos could not follow to convert them.

It seems certain that the river Pescadores, as well as those of St. Joachim and Jesus Maria, which fall into it, take their rise in the icy mountains, since they flow from the east, and pass through the low lands, where they receive a multitude of smaller streams. On the contrary, the river Sacramento flowing from the north, from quite another region, has its source, according to the Indians of the mission, in a great lake. I myself conjecture, that the Slavianka, which falls into the sea near Ross, is an arm of it.

The many rivers flowing through this fruitful country will be of the greatest use to future settlers. The low ground is exactly adapted to the cultivation of rice; and the higher, from the extraordinary strength of the soil, would yield the finest wheat-harvests. The vine might be cultivated here to great advantage. All along the banks of the river grapes grow wild, in as much profusion as the rankest weeds: the clusters were large; and the grapes, though small, very sweet, and agreeably flavoured. We often ate them in considerable quantities, and sustained no inconvenience from them. The Indians also eat them very voraciously.

The chase furnished us with ample and profitable amusement. An abundance of deer, large and small, are to be met with all over the country, and geese, ducks, and cranes, on the banks of the rivers. There was such a superfluity of game, that even those among us who had never been sportsmen before, when once they took the gun in their hands, became as eager as the rest. The sailors chased the deer very successfully.

When it grew dark, we kindled a large fire, that our hunters, some of whom had lost their way, might recover the camp. In the night we were much disturbed by bears, which pursued the deer quite close to our tents; and by the clear moonlight we plainly saw a stag spring into the river to escape the bear; the latter, however, jumped after him, and both swam down the stream till they were out of sight.

At sunrise, as the wind had fallen a little, we continued our voyage. On the shore we met with a small rattlesnake, which might have been a dangerous neighbour. It was, however, his destiny to become our prize, and enrich the collection of Dr. Eschscholtz. The river now took a north-westerly direction. Its breadth was from two hundred and fifty to three hundred fathoms, independently of numerous branches on the east side, flowing between various small islands. The country on the west bank was of a moderate height; that on the east was low. The power of the current impeded our progress, though our rowers exerted all their strength. As the sun advanced towards the meridian, the north wind also rose again; so that with our utmost efforts we could advance but little, and at noon we were obliged to lay-to again, having proceeded only ten miles the whole day. The latitude on the western shore, where we now landed, was 38° 27', and the longitude 122° 10'.

Here we had reached what proved the termination of our little voyage. The unfavourable state of the weather would not allow of our making any farther progress; and our pilot assured us that at this season the quantity of rain that falls, so much swells the river and strengthens the currents, as to make it impossible to contend with the continually increasing force of the stream. We were therefore compelled to abandon the farther prosecution of these inquiries to some future traveller, whose fate shall lead him hither in summer time, when these obstacles do not exist.

The neighbourhood of our landing-place seemed to have been recently the abode of some Indians. We found a stake driven into the earth, to which a bunch of feathers was attached for a weather-cock; in several places fire had been kindled, as some burning embers still attested. There were also two Indian canoes made of reeds. The pilot gave me the names of two tribes who had formerly dwelt in this region, and probably still wandered in its vicinity—the Tschupukanes, and Hulpunes. We could now see the smoke of their fires rising from the marshy islands, the higher parts of which they inhabit.

The majestic chain of mountains of the Sierra Nevada looked most beautiful from this spot. The whole eastern horizon was bounded by these masses of ice, and before them the low land lay spread out like a verdant sea. From the Bay of St. Francisco, the Sierra Nevada are nowhere visible; but they first come in sight after having passed the point where the Pescadores and the Sacramento unite.

The day was again passed in sport, and we shot many stags, the meat of which proved extremely good. During the night we were again disturbed by the little wolves so common here: they stole some pieces of our venison. Early the next morning we prepared for our return, and soon quitted these lovely and fertile plains, where many thousand families might live in plenty and comfort, but which now, from their utter loneliness, leave a mournful impression on the mind, increased by the reflection that the native Indians have been nearly exterminated. During our return voyage, we were very diligent in taking soundings, and found the water in the middle of the river always as much as from fifteen to seventeen and twenty fathoms; but at its mouth not more than four or five fathoms deep.

On the 23rd of November we again reached our vessel, laden with venison for the whole crew. Captain Lasaref had arrived during our absence with his frigate; having struggled with storms almost the whole way from New Archangel to St. Francisco. With the intention of sending letters home by him, I had waited for his arrival to leave California. Our vessel was therefore now immediately prepared for sailing, our camp on shore broken up, and all the instruments brought on board. During the last night our people passed on land, they killed a polecat which had slunk into the tent. This animal, of the size and form of an ordinary cat, has so abominable a smell, that its vicinity is insupportable. Dogs, when they sometimes attack and bite these creatures, cannot relieve themselves from the stench, but continue to rub their noses so violently against the ground as they run, that they leave a stream of blood on their track. Polecats may be considered in the brute creation what the Kalushes are among men.

On the morning of the 25th of November, as soon as the tide ebbed, we towed out of the Bay of St. Francisco with a north-west wind, which here regularly brings fine weather. The sea was still so much agitated by the recent south-west storms, that it rolled large billows into the channel which unites it with the bay. Our vessel being dashed against these breakers by the force of the current from the channel, would no longer obey the helm, and we narrowly escaped being cast against a rock. I would therefore recommend others of my profession only to sail out of this bay when the water in the channel is tranquil, which usually happens after the wind has blown for several days from the north-west.

According to repeated observations, we found the latitude of the Presidio of St. Francisco to be 37° 48' 33", and the longitude 122° 22' 30". The declination of the needle was 16° east.

The medium of our observations in the bay gave us the time for high water, at the new and full moon, 11 hours and 20 minutes.

The greatest difference in the height of the water was seven feet. The rivers which fall into the bay have a great influence on the times of ebb and flow, so that the ebb lasts eight hours, and the flood only four.

THE SANDWICH ISLANDS

On losing sight of the Californian coast, we steered southwards, to take advantage as soon as possible of the trade-wind, proposing by its means to sail direct for the Sandwich Islands. A strong and lasting north-wester favoured our intention, and on the 3rd of December we crossed the tropic of Cancer in the latitude 133° 58', gained the trade-wind, and began our run westward, supposing ourselves secure from storms in this tropical region; we were, however, mistaken: already on the 5th a high wind from the south-east compelled us to take in all sail; on the 6th it shifted to the west, and on the 7th to the north. We experienced from this quarter some violent gusts, after which the heavens cleared, the storm abated, and towards evening on the 8th, we regained the ordinary trade-wind. I mention these storms, only because they are almost unexampled at so great a distance from land, between the tropics, and especially as coming from the west; but it appears that this year was quite out of the ordinary course, and produced a number of strange phenomena of which we heard complaints wherever we went.

The weather, after treating us so ill, again became friendly, and the remainder of our voyage proceeded swiftly and favourably under the magnificent tropical sky: agreeable it was sure to be; for the peculiar charm of a sail between the tropics is appreciated by all seamen. An old English captain, with whom I became acquainted during this voyage, assured me that he could imagine no greater luxury for the remainder of his life, than to possess a good quick-sailing ship, to keep a good table, and to sail between the tropics, without ever making land. I cannot, I confess, altogether participate in this true seaman-like taste: on my voyages, the mere sight of land has always been my great source of pleasure. The conduct of a vessel through distant seas, and through its conflicts with the variable element, is not indeed an uninteresting occupation; but the object which has always chiefly attracted my inclinations, is an intimate knowledge of various countries and their inhabitants; and I have always considered the time spent at sea, as a necessary hardship submitted to with this reward in view. Perhaps I was not born for a sailor: an accident, by no means calculated upon in my previous education, made me such in my fifteenth year.

We sailed in the night past O Wahi, the principal of the Sandwich group, with its celebrated giant mountain Mou-na-roa. At break of day on the 13th, we saw in the west the elevated island of Muwe, and continued our course along the northern shore of this and its neighbour Morotai, to Wahu, where we intended to land. The landscape of a tropical country is always pleasing, even when, as here, high lava hills, and masses of sometimes naked rocks piled like towers upon each other, form the principal features of the coast, at first inspiring the navigator with doubts of its fertility. But how agreeably is he surprised, on reaching the southern shores of these islands, to meet with the most smiling scenery, and most luxuriant vegetation. In the middle of the channel, between the islands Muwe and Morotai, lie two small uninhabited islands, which, strange to say, are not marked on Vancouver's map. We took some pains to ascertain their exact situation.

At four o'clock in the afternoon, the high yellow rock which forms the eastern point of the island of Wahu, became plainly visible above our horizon. We could not reach the secure harbour of Hanaruro, which lies on the southern side of this promontory, before nightfall, and therefore thought it advisable to lay-to between the islands Wahu and Morotai. In the morning, after doubling the conical mountain called the Diamond Mountain, we suddenly came in sight of the harbour, containing a number of ships decorated with the flags of various nations.

I must here make a few remarks for the benefit of such navigators as are not well acquainted with these waters. Whoever wishes to sail in between the islands of Wahu and Morotai, must remember, that throughout the year a strong current always sets here towards the north-west; and that the eastern point of Wahu should be doubled within the distance of three miles from the coast; as farther out to sea, calms are very prevalent here, whilst in the neighbourhood of the land, a fresh breeze regularly sets, in the morning, from the land, and from noon till evening from the sea.

Behind its harbour, safely sheltered by the coral reefs, lies the town of Hanaruro, consisting of irregular rows of dwellings scattered over an open plain. Here and there among the huts are seen houses built of stone in the European fashion. The former lie modestly concealed, under the cooling shade of palm-trees; the latter stand boldly forward, braving the burning sunbeams and dazzling the eye by their overpowering whiteness. Close to the shore the fortress rears its strong turreted walls in a quadrangular form, planted with cannon, and bearing the striped national flag of the Sandwich Islands. The country above the town rises in an amphitheatre, planted with tarro-root, sugar-cane, and banana, and the view to landward is bounded by precipitous mountains invading the clouds, and thickly overgrown with fine trees. In this beautiful panorama we see at once that the island of Wahu deserves the appellation it has acquired,—of the garden of the Sandwich Islands.

As we approached the harbour, I made the usual signal for a pilot, and we soon after saw a boat of European construction making towards us; it was rowed by two naked *Kanachas*, as the lower class of people are here called, the pilot sitting at the rudder in an European dress. When he came on board, I recognised him for the Englishman, Alexander Adams, who on my former voyage in the Rurik had commanded the ship Kahumanna, belonging to King Tameamea; he was now chief pilot. The wind did not immediately allow us to run into the harbour, but in a few hours it became favourable, and our skilful pilot guided us safely through the intricacies of its narrow entrance. Our ship was the largest that had ever passed through this channel, which would be impracticable for first-rate vessels.

Some of the ships we found in the harbour were English and American whalers, which had put in here for provisions; others were on trading voyages to the north-west coast of America for skins, or returning thence with their cargoes. Some were from Canton, laden with Chinese produce, which finds a good market in the Sandwich Islands; and one was a French ship from Bordeaux, which having carried a cargo of iron wares to Chili, Peru, and Mexico, had brought the remains of it here. All the captains visited me in the hope of hearing news from Europe; but many of them had left it later than we had, and accommodated us with their London newspapers.

If we consider that scarcely fifty years have elapsed since these islands were first introduced by Captain Cook to the knowledge of the European public, and that the inhabitants were then completely what we call savages, that is, that they were wholly destitute of any conception of the arts, sciences, or habits of civilized life, we shall find with surprise that the harbour of Hanaruro already bears a character almost entirely European, reminding us only by the somewhat scanty clothing of the natives, of the briefness of their acquaintance with our customs.

My readers, I think, will take some interest in a short account of this people, whose rapid progress in civilization would perhaps by this time have placed them on a level with Europeans, if unfavourable circumstances had not thrown obstacles in the way of their improvement, which it will require another such governor as Tameamea to overcome.

The eleven islands named by Cook after his patron, the Earl of Sandwich, but for which the natives have no common appellation, lie between the nineteenth and twenty-second degrees of north latitude. They are all high and volcanic. O Wahi, the most easterly, and by much the largest, is eighty-seven miles long and seventy-five broad: it has three mountains, which may well bear a comparison with the highest in the world. The climate of these islands is particularly beautiful and healthy.

Their population is estimated by Captain King at four hundred thousand; whose colour, form, language, and manners, testify their relationship with the other islanders of this great ocean, though they have very little knowledge of them. Their earliest history consists of traditions of truths interwoven with fables, which ascend to the first peopling of the islands, and are not yet embodied in the relation of any voyage. I have collected them carefully from the accounts of the most distinguished and intelligent man in Hanaruro, my friend Karemaku, a Spaniard named Marini, who had long resided here, assisting as interpreter.

According to a belief not long ago universally prevalent, the mighty spirit Etua-Rono reigned over these islands before they were inhabited by men. Ardently desirous of seeing his country peopled, he was melancholy, and shed torrents of tears on the mountain Mou-na-roa, because he had no offspring; and his loving wife, the beautiful goddess Opuna, was not in a situation to console him. At length Fate heard his prayers. On the south-east point of the island of O Wahi two boats were stranded, having on board some families, who brought with them hogs, fowls, dogs, and several edible roots. To the present day are the first footsteps of man on this land to be seen. Rono was at that time absent, catching fish on the northern islands for his wife. The fire-god, his subject, unpropitious to man, taking advantage of this circumstance, made an effort to repulse the new-comers. He approached them with terrible gestures, and asked whence they came. They answered—"We come from a country which abounds in hogs, dogs, cocoa-nuts, and bread-fruit. We were overtaken by a violent storm when on a voyage to visit some neighbours; and the moon changed five times before we reached this land." They then begged permission to remain, which the fire-god cruelly refused, and continued inexorable, although they offered to sacrifice a hog to him.

Rono, however, observing that a strange smell proceeded from O Wahi, suddenly returned, and was greatly surprised at the sight of the men. Encouraged by his friendly deportment, they made their petition to him, relating the harsh treatment they had endured from the fire-god. Rono, enraged at this intelligence, threw the fire-god into the crater Kairuo, on the side of the mountain Mou-na-roa, where he still chafes in vain. The men now lived tranquilly on O Wahi, increased in numbers, and sought, by great sacrifices, to prove their love and thankfulness to their protector, Etua-Rono. To his honour were established the solemn yearly games called Makahiti, in which whoever obtained the victory in running, wrestling, and warlike evolutions, was crowned with a verdant wreath and presided as king over the ensuing feast.

The other islands were gradually peopled from O Wahi; the number of the gods also increased; but they all remained subject to Etua-Rono.

Mankind had enjoyed a long period of peace and content under the beneficent protection of Rono, when their happiness was suddenly disturbed by a distressing occurrence. The goddess Opuna, the beautiful consort of Rono, degraded herself by a clandestine connexion with a man of O Wahi. Her husband, furious on the discovery of his wrongs, precipitated her from the top of a high rock, and dashed her to pieces; but had scarcely committed this act of violence when, in an agony of repentance, he ran wildly about the islands, bestowing blows and kicks on every one he met. The people, astonished at this frantic behaviour of the god, enquired the reason of it; on which, with the bitterest expression of grief, he exclaimed, "I have murdered her who was dearest to me!" He bore the remains of Opuna into the Marai on the Bay of Karekakua, and there remained a long time sunk in the deepest grief. At length he determined to quit the islands, where every thing reminded him of the happiness he had enjoyed with his beloved wife. The people were overwhelmed with sorrow by the communication of his intention; and he endeavoured to console them with the promise that he would one day return on a floating island, furnished with all that man could desire, and make his favourite people happy. He then embarked in a vessel of peculiar construction, and set sail for a distant country.

With Rono's departure terminated the Golden Age of this island. Wars and tumults arose; the gods still increased in number; but their influence was no longer so friendly to man as when they were under the superintendence of the revered Rono. Now also commenced many evil customs, such as human sacrifices, which had been unknown in the good old time: cannibalism, however, does not appear ever to have disgraced them. A long period elapsed, of which no record remains; and the story is resumed at the landing of five white men in Karekakua Bay, near to the Marai, where the body of the goddess Opuna reposed. The inhabitants supposed them to be superior beings, and offered no opposition when they proceeded to take possession of the Marai, on which holy place they were not only exempted from persecution, but also by the offerings daily placed there before the images of the gods, from any danger of suffering a scarcity of food. Here, then, they lived very comfortably; and from their having, immediately on their arrival, taken up their abode in the Marai, the people, who were all acquainted with the story of Opuna, concluded they were sent thither by Rono, to watch over the grave of his beloved consort. To this opinion they were indebted for a veneration greater than that entertained for the gods themselves. The priests alone had the privilege of providing for their wants, which they did with the utmost care: the people were not even allowed to approach the neighbourhood of the Marai.

The white men, however, soon found their time hang heavy in this entire seclusion, and formed a more intimate connexion with the priests, whom they assisted in the holy rites and ceremonies, and at length even made their appearance among the people: the latter then discovered them to be mortals like themselves, differing only in colour, but still retained a high respect for their superior knowledge and good deportment. Maidens of the highest rank were given to them for wives; and each of them was installed governor of an island. "The descendants of these strangers," said Karemaku, "may still be distinguished by their whiter colour." Here, as at Tahaiti, the Yeris differ from the lower classes in their superior size, and some also by a greater degree of fairness.

The helmets and short mantles which Cook and King have described as worn by this people, were introduced by these white strangers. At first, the kings only appeared in this costume; but in Cook's time it was common also among the Yeris. Now that European fashions have quite banished those of the original inhabitants, it is only preserved and shown to strangers as a relic of the past. The helmet, of wood covered with small red and yellow feathers, and adorned with a plume, perfectly resembles those of the chivalrous knights of yore; and the short mantle, also most ingeniously made with feathers to supply the want of woven stuff, forms a complete representation of the mantles worn by those ancient heroes: hence it is sufficiently evident that the white men who landed on O Wahi were Europeans; and that we are therefore more nearly connected with, at least, a part of the inhabitants of the Sandwich Islands, than with the other South Sea islanders.

With the arrival of the white men begins the chronology of O Wahi, from the first white king to Tameamea, making seven successive reigns. During this period, but long before Cook's time, two vessels are said to have been wrecked on the north-east side of O Wahi. Tradition is not unanimous in the account of what became of the crews. According to some, they were lost in the wreck, but others say they were murdered by the natives. My informant, Karemaku, mentioned only one ship, which was seen at a distance; and although the iron anchors found at O Wahi and at Muwe prove that they must have been there, he could give no account of them. It is very probable that the Spaniards, who often made a mystery of their discoveries in the South Seas, already knew of the existence of these islands before their discovery by Cook.

Their authentic history begins with this event, in 1778, when, as has already been mentioned, Cook bestowed on them the name of the First Lord of the Admiralty at that period. They were not then, as now, united under one King; but each island had its particular sovereign, called Yeri-Rahi, who possessed full power over the lives of his subjects, and to whom the proprietors of land paid tribute. The name of the monarch of O Wahi, on Cook's arrival, was Teraiopu, or, as he writes it, Terreobu.

Captain King, the companion of Cook, gives the following description of the Sandwich Islanders:—

"They are in general of the middle size,[3] and well-proportioned. Their movements are graceful, they run swiftly, and are able to carry great weights. The men, however, are inferior to the Friendly Islanders, in strength and activity; and the women are not so delicately formed as those of Tahaiti: their colour is also a little browner, and they are not so handsome, but the features of both sexes are open and agreeable; the females especially have beautiful eyes and teeth, and a sweet expression of countenance. Their hair is dark-brown, not so smooth as that of the American Indians, nor so woolly as that of the negroes of Africa, but between the two.

"Here, as on the other South Sea Islands, the Yeris are advantageously distinguished in form from the lower classes, and are seldom disfigured by the swellings and ulcers frequent among the latter, which we ascribed to the great use of salt in their preparations of meat and fish; the former, however, are much injured by immoderate indulgence in the Ava drink. Those who suffered most from it had their whole bodies covered with a white eruption: their eyes were red and inflamed, they trembled much, and could scarcely hold up their heads. This beverage does not shorten the lives of all who use it too freely, as Teraiopu, Kau, and several other chiefs addicted to it, were old men; but it brings on premature and diseased old age. Fortunately, this luxury is the exclusive privilege of the chiefs. The son of Teraiopu, a boy of twelve years old, often boasted of having obtained the right of drinking Ava, and showed with much complacency a spot on his loins where the eruption was already visible.

"Notwithstanding the great and irreparable loss which the sudden violence of these Sandwich Islanders has occasioned us," (in the death of Cook,) "I must in justice declare, that they are usually gentle and kind, and by no means so changeable and volatile as the Tahaitians, nor so reserved and melancholy as the Friendly Islanders: they live on the best possible terms with each other, and in peace and kindness in their families. We have often admired the care and tenderness with which the women treated their children, while the men assisted them in their domestic occupations with a readiness and good-will which did them great credit.

"If however we should pronounce on the degree of civilization to which they have attained by the estimation the female sex enjoys among them, they would rank but low in the scale. The women are not only forbidden to eat with the men, but the best kinds of food are denied them. They are not allowed to eat pork, turtle, or several kinds of fish and bananas; and we were informed that a poor girl had been severely beaten for having tasted of these prohibited viands on board our ship. The females seemed indeed almost to live in a state of separation from their lords; and although we never perceived that they were ill treated, it is certain they are held in little respect.

"We were always received when we came ashore with the greatest friendliness and hospitality. As soon as we landed, the inhabitants vied with each other in bringing us presents, preparing food for us, and showing us every mark of kindness. The old people were much pleased when they obtained permission to touch us; and they showed much modesty and humility in the comparisons they made between us and themselves.

"In mental capacity, the Sandwich Islanders do not appear at all inferior to any other people. Their progress in agriculture, and their skill in handicrafts, is fully proportionate to their means and situation. The earnest attention which they paid to the work of our smiths, and the various means they devised, even before our departure, to give any required form to the iron they obtained from us, convinced us at once of their industry and ingenuity.

"Our unfortunate friend Kancena, (he was shot by one of the Englishmen whom he had always treated with the greatest friendship) had a great desire for knowledge, an admirable natural understanding and a vivacity of mind seldom met with amongst uncultivated nations. He made innumerable inquiries concerning our manners and customs, our King, our form of government, the population and produce of our country, and the manner in which our ships and houses were built. He wished to know if we waged wars, with whom, and for what cause, what God we worshipped, and many other things; which showed an extensive range of thought."

This testimony of Captain King to the good disposition of the Sandwich Islanders becomes the more worthy of credit, when we consider that the English always treated them with great severity, and that Captain Cook only fell a sacrifice to his own error. King has also defended them from the imputation of being cannibals, of which Anderson and several of Cook's companions had accused them.

The propensity to theft was as common among the lower classes here, as on the other South Sea islands; and this it was which occasioned the thoughtless severity of Cook, who was always judge in his own cause, and suffered himself to be hurried into unjustifiable acts of violence. Had he been a philanthropist, as well as a great navigator, he would not have lost his life at O Wahi.

The custom of tattooing existed also among the Sandwich Islanders; their faces were frequently marked with lines crossing each other at right angles, and some even had their tongues tattooed; pretty drawings were frequently seen on the hands and arms of the women. The ordinary dress of both sexes was nothing more than a piece of stuff folded round their bodies. The females adorned themselves besides with necklaces of muscle-shells, or little red shining beans, and with bracelets of various ornamental materials; they sometimes wore collars of beautiful feathers ingeniously blended together; their hair was also decorated with feathers and with garlands of flowers.

The Sandwich Islanders lived in villages or little hamlets of from one to two hundred dwellings, standing irregularly, pretty near each other, and communicating by a winding path. Some of them were surrounded by gardens, enclosed with hedges. The food of the lower classes consisted chiefly of fish, yams, sweet potatoes, tarro-root, bananas, sugar-canes, and bread-fruit. Those of higher rank also indulged in pork, and the flesh of dogs, prepared in the same manner as on the Society Islands. The tame poultry of Europe was also found here, but it was scarce, and not very much prized. These people were particularly clean, and their cookery was preferred by Englishmen to that of their own country.

The Yeris were chiefly employed in the building of vessels and the manufacture of mats; the females prepared a stuff of the paper kind, which was so pressed and coloured as to resemble our calico; and fishing or agriculture was the chief business of the servants. These occupations, however, left leisure for various pastimes, particularly dancing, which the young people of both sexes delighted in. Drums of several sorts were their only musical instruments, but their songs were very pleasing. They often played at a game much resembling our draughts; it is played with black and white stones on a piece of board, and from the great number of pieces, seems to require much attention. In another game, a stone was hidden under a large piece of stuff, and the player was to point out the precise spot in which it lay. Running races, in which the girls took part, and apparently dangerous exercises in swimming amidst the surf, were also among their amusements. In wrestling and boxing, they did not display so much strength and skill as the Friendly Islanders. The children often handled their balls with great dexterity, throwing several at once into the air and catching them again.

Their vessels were very well built; the largest, a double one, seventy feet long, twelve broad, and three and a half deep, belonged to Teraiopu. The most remarkable of their utensils were the vessels appropriated to drinking Ava; they were usually eight or ten inches in diameter, perfectly round and very well polished, and were supported by three or four little images of men in various attitudes, sometimes bearing the vessel on their heads, sometimes on their shoulders, or on their hands raised above their heads. These figures were very well executed, the proportions correctly preserved, and even the proper action of the muscles well defined.

Among the arts in which the Sandwich Islanders excelled, was that of preparing salt: the English obtained from them a large quantity of the best kind. Their arms consisted of clubs, lances, and daggers, made of hard wood. War was of frequent occurrence amongst the inhabitants of the several islands; the battles were often very bloody, and usually at sea, the vessels grappling. The Yeris, when they went to battle, wore the decorated helmets already described, and the mantles covered with black, red, and yellow feathers: those of the Yerirahis, or kings, were of yellow only. Images of the god of war, cut in wood; dreadful caricatures of the human figure in a threatening posture, the mouth open and armed with dogs' teeth, were always carried before the kings into battle; and the chief aim of the enemy was to capture them, as this achievement usually put an end to the war. A part of the prisoners were sacrificed to the gods; but as the shedding of blood in this rite was forbidden, they were strangled, and laid down before the images of the gods in the Marai, with their faces turned to the earth.

The burial of the dead was a very sacred ceremony, and accompanied with many forms. The corpse was laid in a pit till the flesh decayed, the bones were then cleaned, and a part of them distributed among the relations and friends to be preserved as relics, part laid in consecrated ground. Dying persons sometimes desired that their bones should be thrown into the crater of the volcano at O Wahi, which was inhabited by the revered god Pelai. It has already been mentioned, that the women were prohibited from eating many kinds of food; they were also forbidden, under pain of death, to enter a house where the men were eating, and they were entirely secluded from the Marais; with these exceptions, they enjoyed great freedom, and even had a voice in the deliberations concerning war and peace.

The religious regulation of the Tabu, or interdict, existed here as well as on many other of the South Sea islands. A person declared under a Tabu was inviolable; a piece of land under a Tabu must not be trodden by any one; nor must a species of animal so declared, be injured or shot until the Tabu was again taken off. Thus Tameamea declared the diamond mountain under the Tabu, because an Englishman, finding there a piece of quartz-crystal, considered it to be diamond; and the King, finding these were of great value, supposed he possessed in the mountain an inexhaustible treasure, till he discovered his mistake, and the Tabu was taken off.

The vessels first seen by the Sandwich Islanders must have been very small, for when Cook's appeared, they took her for a swimming island, and believed that Etua-Rono, for whom they always retained the most profound veneration, had at length fulfilled his promise and returned to them. The joy was universal; and it was determined to receive the beneficent god, so long absent, who was to restore the Golden Age upon the island, with all possible honours. Neither Cook nor his companion seemed to have had any notion that they were saluted with divine honours; but they considered the ceremonies enacted by the rejoicing people as marks of distinction commonly bestowed on persons of importance. His being called by them "O Rono," (the Rono) did not enlighten him on the subject, as he was unacquainted with the tradition; but he contented himself with the conjecture, that the appellation was a title of honour, signifying chief or priest. Had the conduct of Cook made it possible for the islanders to retain their beneficial error, the good understanding between them and the English would never have been interrupted; but he himself was the first to convince them that he could not be their divine benefactor.

Some of the populace conceived themselves entitled to appropriate a portion of the presents which Rono, according to his promise, had brought them—a licence which was immediately punished by Cook with great severity: the offenders taken in the fact were whipped; those who fled were fired upon; and several persons, some of whom were innocent, lost their lives. Rono could not be so cruel and unjust; and *Tute*, as they called Cook, immediately sunk in their estimation to the rank of ordinary mortals. He was henceforth feared as a mighty chief, but venerated no longer. This change of sentiment was very evident when he returned hither from his voyage northward. The islanders met the ship as before, with hogs and fruits; but they set a price upon them, instead of presenting them, as formerly, in the character of offerings, and accepting the returns made them as gratuitous gifts. Finding that they obtained what appeared to them an exorbitant price for their provisions, they supposed the strangers to come from a land of scarcity for the mere purpose of satisfying their appetites; and the common people wholly ceasing to regard them with reverence, became bolder in their depredations. The King, the Priests, and many of the principal Yeris, still however continued firm in their attachment to the English. A Yeri, named Parea, gave a striking proof of this kindly disposition, which Captain King has thus related:—Some Kanackas, having stolen certain articles, were pursued with muskets; and though every thing was recovered, an English officer thought himself justified in taking possession of a canoe lying on the shore belonging to Parea, who, being perfectly innocent of the theft, reclaimed his property. The officer refused to surrender it; and in the subsequent contest, Parea received so violent a blow on the head with an oar, that he fell senseless to the ground. In the mean time the islanders had assembled, and, irritated at this undeserved outrage on a chief, began to throw stones at the English, who were obliged to swim to a neighbouring rock for safety. The victorious people, thus left in possession of the field of battle, fell upon the English boat, which they would have destroyed but for the interposition of Parea, who had now recovered his senses. He dispersed the crowd, made a signal to the English that they might return, restored their boat, and sent them back in it to their ship. Parea afterwards followed them, taking with him a midshipman's hat, and some other trifles which were missing; expressed his sorrow for the dispute that had arisen, and inquired whether O Rono desired his death, or whether he might come again to the ship.—(It appeared from this that he still looked upon Cook as the deity, or at least affected this belief to propitiate the English.)—He was assured that he had nothing to fear, and would always be welcome; he then touched the nose of the officers, in sign of amity and reconciliation, and returned to land.

Since Parea had hindered his countrymen from wreaking their vengeance on one boat, they indemnified themselves by stealing another, and in the night cut through the rope which fastened it to the ship. Cook, enraged at this occurrence, determined to bring the King himself on board his ship, and detain him there as a hostage till the boat should be restored; a measure which on another island he had already successfully adopted on a similar occasion. He therefore went ashore with a party of soldiers well armed, having given orders that none of the boats belonging to the natives should be suffered to leave the bay, as it was his determination, in case gentler measures should prove ineffectual, to destroy them all. All the boats of both ships, well manned and armed, were therefore so placed as to enforce obedience to this command.

Cook was received, according to King's account, with the greatest respect: the people prostrated themselves before him. He proceeded direct to the old King, and invited him on board his ship. The King immediately consented; but some of the Yeris endeavoured to dissuade him; and the more earnestly Cook pressed his going, the more strenuously they endeavoured to prevent it. Cook, at length, seized the King by the arm, and would have carried him off by force; which in the highest degree irritated the assembled multitudes. At this moment a Yeri, who in crossing the bay from the opposite side had been fired upon by the English boats, rushed with blood streaming from his wound into the presence of the King, and cried aloud to him to remain where he was, or he would certainly receive similar treatment; this incident wound up the rage of the people to its utmost pitch, and the conflict commenced, in which Cook lost his life.

Karemaku, who, when a young man, had witnessed these circumstances, related them to me; and the accounts of Cook's companions upon the whole agree with his. Some isolated facts are differently stated by them; but I was assured by all the natives of Wahu, that Karemaku had strictly adhered to the truth. Even if we give entire credit to the English narrative, we shall find that they were the aggressors,—that the islanders acted only on the defensive, and that Cook's fate, however lamentable, was not entirely undeserved.

John Reinhold Forster, in his preface to a journal of a voyage of discovery to the South Sea, in the years 1776 to 1780, gives an extract from a letter written to him by an Englishman in a responsible situation, in which he says of Cook—"The Captain's character is not the same now as formerly: his head seems to have been turned." Forster gives the same account concerning the change in Cook, when he says—

"Cook, on his first voyage, had with him Messrs. Banks and Solander, both lovers of art and science. On the second, I and my son were his companions, enjoying daily and familiar intercourse with him. In our presence, respect for his own character restrained him; our mode of thinking, our principles and manners influenced his, and prevented his treating the poor harmless South Sea Islanders with cruelty. The only instance of undue severity we ever witnessed in his behaviour, was when on account of some petty theft he once allowed his cannon to be fired upon the fugitive offenders; fortunately, however, no one was injured by this rash act. But having in his last voyage no other witnesses of his actions, than such as were entirely under his command, he forgot what he owed to his own great name, and was guilty in many instances of extreme cruelty. I am therefore convinced, that if Messrs. Banks and Solander, Dr. Spaarmann, or I and my son, had been with him on the last voyage, his life would not have been lost in the manner it was."

The first ships which visited the Sandwich Islands after Cook's death were those of Meeres, Dickson, and Coke, in the years 1786–9. They traded in skins between China and the North-west Coast of America, and found these islands very convenient to touch at. They were well received; and some of the islanders made the voyage to America with them. Tianna, one of the first Yeris of O Wahi, went with Meeres to China. These voyages, and the continual intercourse with Europeans, which their increasing trade in fur produced, necessarily enlarged the ideas of these children of Nature; and as they were not under the dominion of that folly which, in common with the Greenlanders, possesses some of the most civilized nations in Europe, of considering themselves the first people upon earth, they soon acquired our manners, and derived all the advantage that could be expected from the opportunities of improvement thus afforded them. Vancouver found, in 1792, that many remarkable changes had taken place on these islands since Cook's time.

King Teraiopu did not long survive that eminent navigator. His son Kawarao succeeded to the government of the greater part of the island of O Wahi; the rest fell to his relation Tameamea. Kawarao was a tyrant, and governed with unexampled cruelty. At certain periods of the moon, he declared himself holy, or under a Tabu: the priests alone had then the privilege of seeing him so long as the sun was above the horizon; and an immediate death of the severest torture was the melancholy lot of any individual not belonging to this sacred order, who by whatever accident should cast but a momentary glance upon the voluntarily secluded monarch. To this cruelty of disposition, Kawarao united an unbounded ambition, which prompted him to make war on his kinsman Tameamea. This young and powerful chief early distinguished himself, and soon became celebrated throughout these islands for superiority of intellect and skill in arms. Kawarao, although he had greatly the advantage in numbers, could never obtain a victory; fire-arms were not then in use here, and success long vibrated between the contending rivals. Both parties at length determined to put the final issue of the war to the test of a single combat, stipulating that the conqueror should acquire the sovereignty of the whole island. The two kings armed; their respective priests carried the images of their gods to the field, and the fight commenced. Kawarao trusted to his skill in throwing the javelin; but Tameamea could defend himself from several antagonists at once, and scarcely ever missed his aim. After some fruitless efforts of both combatants, Tameamea's spear pierced the side of his bloodthirsty enemy, who fell dead on the field.

This duel, by which Tameamea became King of O Wahi and of Muwe, which had also belonged to Kawarao, took place in the year 1781. To establish his dominion on a firmer basis, Tameamea married the daughter of the vanquished monarch, and acquired the love of his subjects by his wise and moderate government. Himself endowed with uncommon powers of mind, he entrusted the important offices of state only to such as were capable of discharging them efficiently. He made a very fortunate choice in Karemaku, who, while quite a young man, entered into all the enlightened and comprehensive views of his master, forwarded them with ability and energy, and continued his faithful servant till the death of Tameamea. The English called him the Pitt of the Sandwich Islands.

Several Europeans now established themselves at O Wahi; among whom Davis and John Young have been the most useful to the rising nation. Under their direction, houses and ships have been constructed in the European fashion; the island has been enriched with many useful plants; and their advice has been successfully followed in the affairs of government.

With the appearance of Vancouver, arose the fortunate star of these islands. Among the innumerable benefits he conferred upon them, they are indebted to him for the possession of sheep and cattle. Tameamea declared these animals under a Tabu for ten years, which allowed time for so large an increase, that they now run wild in the forests. Had Vancouver enjoyed Cook's advantages, the islanders might still have believed him their Rono.

Tameamea, during Vancouver's visit, swayed the sceptre only over the islands of O Wahi and Muwe, and was engaged in wars with his neighbour kings, whom he fought with the assistance of cannon purchased from European ships. He commanded in every battle, both by sea and land; and Karemaku, as first in authority under him, was his constant companion. The O Wahians, however, could not have well understood the use of their cannons and other fire-arms, as, after Vancouver's departure, the war was maintained for ten years. O Tuai, the most north-westerly island, even then held out, though the others had submitted. In the year 1817, Tameamea conquered this also, after many unsuccessful attempts, and thus became the supreme governor of the whole Archipelago.

From this time all his efforts were directed to the education of his people, and the improvement of their trade. Salt and sandal-wood were the chief articles of exportation. The latter, though bought at rather a high price by the North-American ships, which almost exclusively monopolized this trade, sold for a large profit at Canton.

I have been told, that the Americans have purchased sandal-wood here to the amount of three hundred thousand Spanish dollars a-year. Tameamea bartered this wood for some large American merchant-ships, manned them, and other ships built in the Sandwich Islands, partly with his own subjects, and partly with Europeans, and traded on his own account. He had even found means to create a small fleet of ships of war; and his warehouses, built of stone, were filled with European and American merchandise. He possessed a considerable treasure in silver money and utensils; his fortresses were planted with cannon of a large calibre, and he maintained a force of fifteen thousand men, all armed with muskets, in the use of which they had been carefully exercised. He took much pains, assisted by the Spaniard Marini, to introduce the cotton-tree, which answered very well, and yielded fine cotton; and endeavoured to improve the native flax, already much superior to that of New Zealand, and to profit by it as an article of commerce. Nothing which promised advantage to his country escaped his penetrating mind; he exerted, in short, every faculty of his mind to place the Sandwich Islands in a state of progressive assimilation to the most prosperous nations. Vessels of every nation were as secure from injustice or insult in his ports, as in those of Europe, if not more so. As soon as a strange ship arrived, criers were employed to give notice that the new comers were friends, and must be hospitably received, and that any incivility shown them would be severely punished.

When Tameamea first sent a ship to Canton with sandal-wood, he was obliged to pay a considerable duty for anchorage; whereupon he argued, that what was exacted from himself, he might with a safe conscience demand from others; and every ship is now required to pay forty Spanish dollars for anchorage in the outer, and eighty in the inner harbour of Hanaruro.

Wahu is the most fertile of all the islands, and the only one enjoying a secure harbour; it therefore naturally advances the most rapidly in civilization. Several European and American traders have settled in Hanaruro; shops have been opened, and houses built in the European style, of wood and stone; some of the former were made in America, and brought here to be put together. The exertions of Marini introduced here many European vegetables, the vine and other fruits, which are all in a flourishing state. He collected and tamed a herd of cows. Goats, sheep, and poultry of all kinds are common. The frequent voyages which the Sandwich islanders now made, partly in Tameamea's vessels, partly foreign ones, on board which they served as sailors, gradually familiarised them with the manners of more civilized nations. They adopted our costume, but after the Tahaitian fashion; considering a complete suit as an unnecessary luxury. Even Tameamea himself, for his usual attire, wore only a shirt, trowsers, and red waistcoat, without a coat; he possessed, however, many richly embroidered uniforms, but kept them for grand occasions.

These islanders had made great progress in the English language: many of them could speak it very tolerably. Tameamea understood, but did not speak it. If any of my readers should wish for a farther acquaintance with the character of this distinguished sovereign, I must refer them to Vancouver, and to my former voyage; but for the benefit of those who may not be disposed to take this trouble, I cannot forbear repeating from the latter some of his remarks to myself. He presented me with a collar most ingeniously worked with coloured feathers, which he had sometimes worn in war, and on solemn occasions, saying, "I have heard that your monarch is a great warrior, and I love him, because I am a warrior myself; bear to him this collar, which I send as a token of my regard." Once as he embraced an image in his Marai, he said, "These are our Gods whom I adore; whether in so doing I am right or wrong, I know not, but I follow the religion of my country, which cannot be a bad one, since it commands me to be just in all my actions."

On the 8th of May, in the year 1819, Tameamea terminated his meritorious career, to the great sorrow as well of the foreign settlers as of his native subjects. His remains were disposed of according to the rites of the religion he professed. After they had remained some time in the Marai, the bones were cleaned, and divided among his relatives and the most distinguished of his attendants. According to the custom of this country, two persons had long before been destined for interment with him at his death; but by his express desire this ceremony was dispensed with.

His eldest son and legitimate successor, Lio Lio, or, as the English call it, *Rio Rio*,—for there is some difficulty in distinguishing between the L and the R of the Sandwich Islanders,—now assumed the government, under the name of Tameamea the Second. Unhappily, the father's talents were not hereditary; and the son's passion for liquor incapacitated him for ruling with the same splendid reputation an infant state, which, having already received so strong an impulse towards civilization, required a skilful guide to preserve it from degeneracy and error.

The chiefs of some of the islands, and especially of O Tuai, had, even in Tameamea's lifetime, founded a hope of future independence, on the weakness of his successor, and immediately upon his death proceeded to attempt the accomplishment of their desires. But Karemaku, the faithful friend and counsellor of the deceased King, to whom the whole nation looked up with affection, and whose penetration easily discerned the evil consequences that would ensue from a political disunion of the islands, devoted to the son all the zeal and patriotism with which he had served the father. By the influence of his eloquence, and the force of his arms, he quelled the insurrection, and re-established peace and order; but to enthrone the new monarch in the hearts of his people exceeded his ability; and their disaffection proved that the germ of future disorders was not wholly extinct. The King chose Wahu for his residence, because this island was in the best state for defence; and giving himself up entirely to dissipation, sunk lower and lower in the estimation of his subjects. Karemaku was the good genius who watched over the welfare of the country, while its monarch was wasting his hours and his health in orgies, at which he was frequently known to empty a bottle of rum at a draught. It was not to be supposed that a king addicted to such habits should conceive any projects of utility or advantage for his people; he wished, however, to distinguish himself by some effort in their favour, or at least to relieve them from the trammels of superstition. He was a freethinker in a bad sense. He hated the religion of his country, because it laid some restraints upon his inclinations, and he determined to overthrow it; not for the purpose of introducing a better, a task to which his feeble mind was unequal, but for that of at once relieving himself and his subjects from ceremonies which he considered useless, because he undervalued the precepts of morality interwoven with them, and for the sake of which his father had always conscientiously observed them.

In the fifth month of his reign, he proceeded in a violent and brutal manner, notwithstanding all the remonstrances of Karemaku, to the execution of his design. Having previously arranged his plans with some chiefs, the companions of his excesses, he invited the principal inhabitants of the islands to a sumptuous banquet. After the wine and rum had produced their wonted effects, females were introduced, and compelled to partake of the feast. These poor creatures, having no suspicion of the King's intentions, shrunk with terror from a profanation punishable with death. But their resistance was unavailing: they were not only constrained to sit down to the repast in company with the men, but even to eat pork; and thus, to the great astonishment of such guests as were not in the secret, to violate, at the royal command, a double Tabu. A murmur arose; but the greater part of the company were under the influence of liquor, and the King now openly proclaimed his intentions. His auditors inquired in alarm what crime the Gods had committed, that they should be thus unceremoniously dismissed; and besought him not to occasion his own destruction and that of the country, by provoking their indignation. The King started from his seat, and exclaimed with violent gestures, "You see we have already violated the strongest Tabus, and yet the Gods inflict no punishment, because they have no power; neither have they power to do us good. Our faith was erroneous and worthless. Come, let us destroy the Marais, and from henceforth acknowledge no religion!" The immediate dependents of the King rose to second him: the inhabitants of Hanaruro had been depraved by their intercourse with foreign sailors, and a tumultuous crowd, who held nothing sacred, soon followed the revellers. Arrived at the royal Marai, some of them, terrified by the aspect of their idols, would have receded; but when the King himself, and his friends and followers, began to maltreat them, and no divine vengeance followed, the courage of the multitude revived, and the Marais were soon utterly destroyed. This outrage to what the people at large most venerated, introduced a scene of confusion and violence, and would indeed have entailed destruction both on the King and the country, had not Karemaku again stood forward in their defence. Several Yeris who, disapproving the sentiments of the King, had retired privately from the banquet, joined the priests in exciting the people to defend their gods by force of arms. An army was raised, and, animated by the presence of the war-god, commenced hostilities against his sacrilegious opponents. When the news of the destruction of the Marais reached the other islands, insurrections also broke out in each of them. Karemaku had condemned the sacrilege, and abstained from any part in it; but as it could not now be prevented, and he foresaw the mischievous consequences of civil commotions, he assembled an army, and, victorious wherever he appeared, succeeded in restoring tranquillity. On the large island O Wahi, however, he encountered a formidable resistance; but at length, after several bloody contests, he captured the war-god: the insurgents, who had also lost their leaders in the last battle, believing themselves quite abandoned by the gods, now dispersed, and Karemaku, on the restoration of tranquillity, returned to Wahu.

It is a remarkable fact, that a people who regarded their faith and their priests with so much reverence, as I had myself witnessed previously to this occurrence, should in so short a period, acquiescing in the decree which denounced their creed as error, and consigned their sanctuaries to demolition, contentedly submit to the total deprivation of all external signs of religion. Karemaku had judgment enough to perceive that this state of things would not endure, and that a religion of some kind was indispensable to the people; he therefore resolved to set his countrymen a good example, and yielding to an inclination he had long entertained, to declare himself publicly a convert to Christianity. In the same year, 1819, Captain Freycinet, on his voyage round the world, landed at Hanaruro, and a clergyman accompanying him, Karemaku and his brother Boki received the sacrament of baptism according to the forms of the Catholic Church.

At this time, a society of missionaries was formed in the United States of America, for the purpose of introducing Christianity into the Sandwich Islands. Of the extinction of the ancient faith, which must of course facilitate their undertaking, they had as yet received no information. Six families of these missionaries arrived at Wahu in 1820, bringing with them two young Sandwich Islanders, who had been previously prepared in their schools. The King, hearing of their intention, would not allow them to land, but commanded them immediately to depart from his shores. Here, again, Karemaku interposed, and endeavoured to convince the King that the Christian religion would be one of the greatest benefits he could confer on his subjects. The King then assembled the most distinguished Yeris, and after fourteen days' deliberation, decreed that a piece of land should be granted to the missionaries, with permission to build a church, and to preach their doctrines, under the condition that they should immediately leave the island if the experiment should be found to have a prejudicial influence on the people. The missionaries agreed to the terms, took up their residence on Wahu, and from thence extended settlements over the other islands. Their first efforts were successfully directed to the conversion of the King, his family, and the most distinguished Yeris. When these personages had openly professed the new faith, the Missionaries considered themselves firmly established, and proceeded with more confidence to the full execution of their plan. They quickly acquired the language of the islands, which from the largest of them they called the O Wahi language, printed the first book in it, (a collection of Hymns,) in the year 1822, and instructed the natives, who proved apt scholars, in reading and writing. These missionaries were Protestants; but the Catholic Karemaku, having no notion of the points of doctrine in dispute between the Churches, joined without hesitation in communion with them; and the Christian religion spreading rapidly among the Sandwich Islanders, without any of the constraint or persecution which had disgraced it at O Tahaiti, promised the happiest effects.

Notwithstanding, however, all the efforts of Karemaku, the people were not yet entirely pacified. The former faith had still many secret adherents, and the King was unable to acquire either the esteem or affection of his subjects. Insurrections were continually dreaded; and Rio Rio, not feeling sufficiently secure even in his entrenchments at Wahu, determined, by the advice of some Europeans, to make a voyage to England, in the hope that these discontents would subside during his absence. He confided the administration of the government to the faithful Karemaku, and Kahumanna, the favourite wife of his father, and in the year 1824 sailed for England in a North American ship, accompanied by his consort, Karemaku's brother Boki, and some other persons of rank; taking with him twenty-five thousand Spanish piastres from the treasure amassed by his father.

Soon after the King's departure, a regular rebellion broke out in the island of O Tuai. Its former ruler, Tamari, was dead, and his son, a young man who had been brought up in the United States of America, and had unfortunately fallen into bad company, was desirous to recover for himself the independent dominion of the island. Karemaku and Kahumanna immediately hastened thither with an army, and on our arrival at Hanaruro we found the war still raging at O Tuai, though it was supposed to be near its close. The government of Wahu was entrusted, during the absence of the Regents, to another wife of Tameamea, named Nomahanna, conjointly with a Yeri called Chinau.

On the morning after our arrival, I rowed ashore with some of my officers, to pay my respects to the Queen Nomahanna, and on landing was met by the Spaniard Marini, who accompanied us to her Majesty as interpreter. On the way I was recognised by several old friends, with whom I had become acquainted on my former visit. They saluted me with a friendly "*Aroha.*" I cannot say there was much room for compliment on any visible improvement in their costume; for they still wore with much self-complacency some ill-assorted portions of European attire.

The residence of Nomahanna lay near the fortress on the sea-shore: it was a pretty little wooden house of two stories, built in the European style, with handsome large windows, and a balcony very neatly painted. We were received on the stairs by Chinau, the governor of Wahu, in a curious dishabille. He could hardly walk from the confinement his feet suffered in a pair of fisherman's shoes, and his red cloth waistcoat would not submit to be buttoned, because it had never been intended for so colossal a frame. He welcomed me with repeated "*Arohas*," and led me up to the second floor, where all the arrangements had a pleasing and even elegant appearance. The stairs were occupied from the bottom to the door of the Queen's apartments, by children, adults, and even old people, of both sexes, who, under her Majesty's own superintendence, were reading from spelling-books, and writing on slates—a spectacle very honourable to her philanthropy. The Governor himself had a spelling-book in one hand, and in the other a very ornamental little instrument made of bone, which he used for pointing to the letters. Some of the old people appeared to have joined the assembly rather for example's sake, than from a desire to learn, as they were studying, with an affectation of extreme diligence, books held upside down.

The spectacle of these scholars and their whimsical and scanty attire, nearly upset the gravity with which I had prepared for my presentation to the Queen. The doors were, however, thrown open and I entered, Chinau introducing me as the captain of the newly-arrived Russian frigate. The apartment was furnished in the European fashion, with chairs, tables, and looking-glasses. In one corner stood an immensely large bed with silk curtains; the floor was covered with fine mats, and on these, in the middle of the room, lay Nomahanna, extended on her stomach, her head turned towards the door, and her arms supported on a silk pillow. Two young girls lightly dressed, sat cross-legged by the side of the Queen, flapping away the flies with bunches of feathers. Nomahanna, who appeared at the utmost not more than forty years old, was exactly six feet two inches high, and rather more than two ells in circumference. She wore an old-fashioned European dress of blue silk; her coal-black hair was neatly plaited, at the top of a head as round as a ball; her flat nose and thick projecting lips were certainly not very handsome, yet was her countenance on the whole prepossessing and agreeable. On seeing me, she laid down the psalm-book in which she had been reading, and having, with the help of her attendants, changed her lying for a sitting posture, she held out her hand to me in a very friendly manner, with many "*Arohas!*" and invited me to take a seat on a chair by her side. Her memory was better than my own; she recognised me as the Russian officer who had visited the deceased monarch Tameamea, on the island of O Wahi. On that occasion I had been presented to the Queens; but since that time Nomahanna had so much increased in size, that I did not know her again. She was aware how highly I esteemed her departed consort; my appearance brought him vividly to her remembrance, and she could not restrain her tears, in speaking of his death. "The people," said she, "have lost in him a protector and a father. What will now be the fate of these islands, the God of the Christians only knows." She now informed me with much self-gratulation that she was a Christian, and attended the prayer-meeting several times every day. Desirous to know how far she had been instructed in the religion she professed, I inquired through Marini the grounds of her conversion. She replied that she could not exactly describe them, but that the missionary Bengham, who understood reading and writing perfectly well, had assured her that the Christian faith was the best; and that, seeing how far the Europeans and Americans, who were all Christians, surpassed her compatriots in knowledge, she concluded that their belief must be the most reasonable. "If, however," she added, "it should be found unsuited to our people, we will reject it, and adopt another."

Hence it appears that the christianity of the missionaries is not regarded with the reverence which, in its purity, it is calculated to inspire in the most uncultivated minds. In conclusion, Nomahanna triumphantly informed me, that the women might now eat as much pork as they pleased, instead of being, as formerly, limited to dog's flesh. At this observation, an intrusive idea suddenly changed her tone and the expression of her features. With a deep sigh, she exclaimed—"What would Tameamea say if he could behold the changes which have taken place here? No more Gods—no more Marais: all are destroyed! It was not so in his time:—we shall never have such another king!" Then, while the tears trickled down her cheeks, she bared her right arm, and showed me, tattooed on it in the O Wahi language—"Our good King Tameamea died on the 8th of May 1819." This sign of mourning for the beloved monarch, which cannot be laid aside like our pieces of crape, but accompanies the mourner to the grave, is very frequent on the Sandwich Islands, and testifies the esteem in which his memory is held: but it is a still more striking proof of the universal grief for his loss, that on the anniversary of his death, all his subjects struck out one of their front teeth; and the whole nation have in consequence acquired a sort of whistle in speaking. Chinau had even had the above words tattooed on his tongue, of which he gave me ocular demonstration; nor was he singular in this mode of testifying his attachment. It is surprising that an operation so painful, and which occasions a considerable swelling, should not be attended with worse consequences.

Nomahanna spoke with enthusiasm on the subject of writing. Formerly, she said, she could only converse with persons who were present; now, let them be ever so far distant, she could whisper her thoughts softly to them alone. She promised to write me a letter, in order, she said, that I might prove to every one in Russia that Nomahanna was able to write.

Our conversation was interrupted by the rattling of wheels, and the sound of many voices. I looked from the window, and saw a little cart to which a number of active young men had harnessed themselves with the greatest complacency. I inquired of Marini what this meant, and was informed that the Queen was about to drive to church: an attendant soon after entered, and announced that the equipage was ready. Nomahanna graciously proposed my accompanying her; and rather than risk her displeasure by a refusal, I accepted the invitation with many thanks, though I foresaw that I should thus be drawn in as a party to a very absurd spectacle.

The Queen now put on a white calico hat decorated with Chinese flowers, took a large Chinese fan in her hand, and, having completed her toilette by drawing on a pair of clumsy sailor's boots, we set out. In descending the stairs, she made a sign that the school was over for the present; an announcement that seemed very agreeable to the scholars, to the old ones especially. At the door below, a crowd had assembled, attracted by curiosity to see me and their Queen drive out together. The young men in harness shouted for joy, and patiently waited the signal for the race. Some delay, however, occurred in taking our seats with suitable dignity. The carriage was very small, and my companion very large, so that I was fain to be content with a seat upon the edge, with a very good chance of losing my balance, had not her Majesty, to obviate the danger, encircled my waist with her stout and powerful arm, and thus secured me on my seat; our position, and the contrast presented by our figures, had no doubt a sufficiently comical effect. When we were at length comfortably settled, the Governor Chinau came forth, and with no other addition than a round hat to the costume already described, mounted a meagre unsaddled steed, and off we all went at full gallop, the Queen taking infinite pains to avoid losing me by the way. The people came streaming from all sides, shouting "*Aroha maita!*"—our team continually increasing, while a crowd behind contended for the honour of helping to push us forward. In this style we drove the whole length of Hanaruro, and in about a quarter of an hour reached the church, which lies on an ugly flat, and exactly resembles that at O Tahaiti both in external and internal appearance.

The congregation was very small. Nomahanna and an old lady were the only individuals of their sex; and Chinau, myself, and a few others, the only males present. Even the people who had drawn us did not enter the church; from which I infer, that the influence of the missionaries is by no means so considerable as at O Tahaiti; and certainly the converts are not yet driven with a stick into the house of prayer: nor would it be easy to fasten on the minds of the people the fetters so patiently endured on the Society Islands, where the labours of the missionaries are seldom interrupted by the intervention of strangers. The Sandwich Islanders are engaged in constant intercourse with foreign sailors, mostly of licentious characters, who indeed profess the Christian religion; but brought hither by the desire of gain, or the necessity of laying in provisions for their ships, are generally wholly occupied in driving crafty bargains, and certainly are no way instrumental in inspiring the islanders with ideas of religion or morality, but on the contrary, set them examples which have a direct tendency to deprave their minds. Such among these crews as have been guilty of offences on board ship, frequently run away and settle on the islands. This was severely prohibited in Tameamea's time, but is now permitted, from Christian charity. Such characters as these, reckless of every thing sacred, do not hesitate to make a jest of the missionaries, whose extraordinary plans and regulations offer many weak points to the shafts of ridicule.

When Mr. Bengham had concluded a discourse in the O Wahi language, which might possibly have been highly edifying, but that it was addressed to little else than empty benches,—for I did not understand him, and the minds of the few other persons present were evidently occupied with very different matters,—we returned to the palace in the same style that we had left it. I then took my leave, having received a promise of being amply supplied with provisions: the Queen also, at my request, ordered a small house near her own to be prepared for our astronomical observations, and our astronomer, M. Preus, took possession of it on the following day.

Our arrival had created a great sensation on the island. A foreign ship of war is an uncommon spectacle here—one from Russia more especially, as the attempt of the insane Dr. Scheffer, in 1816, to raise the island of O Tuai against Tameamea, in the hope of annexing it to the empire of Russia, had naturally introduced a fear of similar projects, although the absurd design was entirely discountenanced by the Emperor Alexander. The English also, even in their writings, have contributed to spread the ridiculous idea, that Russia entertained views against the independence of the Sandwich Islands; and that Rio Rio's voyage was only undertaken for the purpose of imploring the assistance of England against our government. From the air of protection which England has for some time past assumed towards these islands, it is probable that she herself secretly harbours such a design, and only waits a favourable opportunity for its execution; although the English always profess to acknowledge the sovereignty of the native monarch, and the King of England, in writing to Tameamea, calls him, "Your Majesty."

I am, however, far from desiring to maintain this opinion as founded on any sufficient grounds. The alarm of the islanders, on the present occasion, had been in great measure excited by a paragraph in a Mexican newspaper, recently imported, which contained a new version of the English fiction. The mistrust, however, did not long subsist. My assurances of friendship, and the particularly good behaviour of the whole crew, by which they were advantageously distinguished from those of the other ships lying here, soon attracted towards us the confidence and esteem of the natives and their governors. During the whole of my stay on the island, I had not the slightest cause to be dissatisfied with the conduct of my men, notwithstanding the temptations to which they were exposed, from the example of other sailors. All that could be spared from the ship were, every Sunday, allowed to go ashore; this being generally known in Hanaruro, a crowd of Wahuaners were always in waiting to welcome the arrival of our boat. The friendly intercourse which at all times subsisted between our people and the islanders was truly gratifying.

I observed with regret, in my daily visits to Hanaruro, that the Wahuaners had lost the simplicity and innocence of character which formerly distinguished them. The profligate habits of the settlers of all nations among them, and of the numerous foreign sailors with whom they constantly associate, have most prejudicially affected their morals. Fraud, theft, and burglary, never heard of in Tameamea's time, are now frequent. Murder implies a degree of wickedness to which they have not yet attained; but a circumstance that occurred shortly before our arrival, may perhaps become an example even for this worst of crimes. The crew of an English whaler, in which much drinking had been permitted, mutinied, and the Captain received a blow on the head, which, though it did not destroy life, produced insanity; nor could all the efforts of our physician wholly restore his reason. He had indeed lucid intervals, during which he became reconciled to his crew, and at length sailed for England; but I have reason to believe the vessel never reached its destination.

One very unpleasant consequence has attended progressive civilization in Hanaruro:—painted signs, that the means of intoxication might be purchased within, hang from many of the houses: their keepers are runaway sailors, who, to increase their own profit, naturally have recourse to every means that may tempt the people to excess; and these liquor-shops accordingly enjoy a constant overflow of visitors. Others are fitted up in a superior style, for the exclusive accommodation of Yeris and ships' officers, admission being refused to Kanackas and sailors. Carousing is here also the order of the day, but billiards and whist form part of the entertainments; the latter game especially is a great favourite with the Wahuaners, who play it well. Whist parties may be seen every where seated on the ground, in the streets or in open fields, among whom large sums of money and valuable goods are at stake. The players are always surrounded by spectators, who pronounce their opinions very volubly at the close of every game. The parties themselves are extremely animated, and the affair seldom terminates without a quarrel. Many other games are also in favour; and through the prevalence of a custom which cannot be observed without regret, this once industrious and flourishing people are rapidly acquiring confirmed habits of idleness and dissipation. A great part of the well cultivated tarro-fields, which formerly surrounded Hanaruro, now lie waste. On the great market-place, horse and foot races are proceeding all day long, and give occasion to extensive gambling. The Wahuaners have as great a passion for horse-racing, as the Malays for cock-fighting, and without hesitation venture their whole stock of wealth on a race. The purchase of a horse is, indeed, the great object of their ambition; and little attention having hitherto been directed to the breeding of these animals, they are imported from California, at an expense of from two to three, or even five hundred piastres; so that many a Wahuaner is obliged to hoard his whole earnings for years together, to raise the means of indulging in this luxury. In these races the horse is not saddled, and a string supplies the place of a bit; the rider is usually quite naked, but very skilful in the management even of the wildest horse; but, as the treatment is injudicious, they are soon worn out.

Large sums are also staked at the *ship-games*, as they are called, in which the islanders display their seaman-like tastes. The players are usually clever ship-builders. They build pretty little vessels, in conformity with the rules of art, and, by their good management of the keel, make them good sailers; they rig them completely, and decorate them with flags and streamers. Then assembling on the banks of some large pond, the owners spread the sails, make the helm fast, and launch the little fleet. The ship which is best built and rigged, first gains the opposite shore, and wins the prize. The spectators take great interest in the game, and a loud shout announces the victory. The children also, in imitation of their fathers, make little ships, and have sailing-matches on the smaller pieces of water.

From the partiality of the Sandwich Islanders for a sea-life, and from their geographical situation, it is probable that, in time, they will become powerful at sea. Tameamea left to his successor above a dozen good ships, all manned with natives. They obtain excellent nautical educations on board the United States' vessels trading between America and Canton; and the Americans, who are equal to the English as seamen, bear witness to the abilities of the islanders.

Luxury has made great advances in Wahu. Even among the lowest class of the people, some article of European clothing is universal. The females especially set their hearts upon the most fashionable mode of dress: whatever the Queen wears is their model, which they imitate to the utmost of their power. The men are importuned to gratify this feminine vanity; and if their means will not enable them to do so fairly, they will often have recourse to fraud. The love of foreign wares, and especially of such as serve for dress and ornament, is by far the most fertile source of crime. The shopkeepers are emulous to make their assortment of goods as attractive as possible, and sometimes allow their customers credit, in which case they never fail to charge double, though their profits are at all times enormous. I have myself seen young girls paying two Spanish dollars for a string of common glass-beads which would scarcely reach round the throat. The tradespeople practise every species of deception with impunity, for the laws are not yet sufficiently civilized to meet offences of this description; which therefore inflict a double injury on their dupe, by robbing him of his property, and affording him an example of successful fraud, which he will generally at least endeavour to imitate. On Sunday, the inhabitants of Wahu make their appearance at church in full dress to be admired; and if the spectacle on these occasions is not so thoroughly laughable as at O Tahaiti, it is certainly sufficiently comic.

The domestic utensils, formerly in use here, have entirely disappeared even from the poorest huts; and Chinese porcelain has superseded the manufactures from the gourd or the cocoa-nut.

Fourteen days after our arrival, I received a message from Karemaku, who was still at O Tuai. He assured me that he was rejoiced at my coming, stated that he had sent orders to Chinau to supply my ship with the best provisions, and added, that having happily concluded the expedition, he should soon return to Hanaruro.

Meanwhile, we had no cause to complain of our situation: every thing was to be had for money; and Nomahanna overwhelmed us with presents of fat hogs and the finest fish, putting all the fishermen into requisition to provide abundantly for our table. We had all reason to be grateful for her attention and kindness, and are all therefore ready to maintain that she is not only the cleverest and the most learned, but also the best woman in Wahu, as indeed she is considered both by the natives and settlers. But I can also bear testimony to another qualification, of equal importance in her estimation—she has certainly the greatest appetite that ever came under my observation. I usually visited her in the morning, and was in the habit of finding her extended at full length upon the floor, employed in inditing her letter to me, which appeared to occasion her many a head-ache. Once, however, I called exactly at dinner-time, and was shown into the eating-room. She was lying on fine mats before a large looking-glass, stretched as usual on her prodigious stomach: a number of Chinese porcelain dishes, containing food of various kinds, were ranged in a semicircle before her, and the attendants were busily employed in handing first one and then another to her Majesty. She helped herself with her fingers from each in its turn, and ate most voraciously, whilst two boys flapped away the flies with large bunches of feathers. My appearance did not at all disturb her: she greeted me with her mouth full, and graciously nodded her desire that I should take my seat in a chair by her side, when I witnessed, I think, the most extraordinary meal upon record. How much had passed the royal mouth before my entrance, I will not undertake to affirm; but it took in enough in my presence to have satisfied six men! Great as was my admiration at the quantity of food thus consumed, the scene which followed was calculated to increase it. Her appetite appearing satisfied at length, the Queen drew her breath with difficulty two or three times, then exclaimed, "I have eaten famously!" These were the first words her important business had allowed her time to utter. By the assistance of her attendants, she then turned upon her back, and made a sign with her hand to a tall, strong fellow, who seemed well practised in his office; he immediately sprang upon her body, and kneaded her as unmercifully with his knees and fists as if she had been a trough of bread. This was done to favour digestion; and her Majesty, after groaning a little at this ungentle treatment, and taking a short time to recover herself, ordered her royal person to be again turned on the stomach, and recommenced her meal. This account, whatever appearance of exaggeration it may bear, is literally true, as all my officers, and the other gentlemen who accompanied me, will witness.

M. Preuss, who lived in the neighbourhood of the lady, frequently witnessed similar meals, and maintains that Nomahanna and her fat hog were the greatest curiosities in Wahu. The latter is in particular favour with the Queen, who feeds him almost to death: he is black, and of extraordinary size and fatness: two Kanackas are appointed to attend him, and he can hardly move without their assistance.

Nomahanna is vain of her tremendous appetite. She considers most people too thin, and recommends inaction as an accelerator of her admired *embonpoint*—so various are the notions of beauty. On the Sandwich Islands, a female figure a fathom long, and of immeasurable circumference, is charming; whilst the European lady laces tightly, and sometimes drinks vinegar, in order to touch our hearts by her slender and delicate symmetry.

One of our officers obtained the Queen's permission to take her portrait. The limner's art is still almost a novelty here; and many persons of rank solicited permission to witness the operation. With the greatest attention, they watched every stroke of the outline, and loudly expressed their admiration as each feature appeared upon the paper. The nose was no sooner traced, than they exclaimed—"Now Nomahanna can smell!" When the eyes were finished—"Now she can see!" They expressed especial satisfaction at the sight of the mouth, because it would enable her to eat;

and they seemed to have some apprehension that she might suffer from hunger. At this point, Nomahanna became so much interested, that she requested to see the picture also: she thought the mouth much too small, and begged that it might be enlarged. The portrait, however, when finished, did not please her; and she remarked rather peevishly—"I am surely much handsomer than that!"

On the 17th of January, Karemaku arrived with a squadron of two and three-masted ships, and many soldiers, before the harbour of Hanaruro, after having terminated the war at O Tuai quite to his satisfaction. The fleet being unable to enter the harbour, on account of a contrary wind, was obliged to cast anchor outside. I immediately sent off an officer with my shallop, to convey to the King's deputy my congratulations on his arrival; he and his young wife (his wife, of whom I spoke in my former voyage, was since dead,) returned in the shallop, and came on board my ship. I fired a salute as he approached, which pleased him much, as he said this compliment from a Russian ship of war would tend to remove from the minds of his countrymen their injurious suspicions of the intentions of Russia.

Karemaku seemed sincerely glad to see me again, and, after a most cordial embrace, presented his young and pretty wife to me. He minutely examined all parts of the ship, expressed his approbation of much that was new to him, and at length exclaimed—"How wide a difference there still is between this ship and ours!—would that they could be made to resemble it! O, Tameamea, thou wast taken from us too soon!" In my cabin, he spoke of the death of his royal friend in terms which Marini declared it impossible to translate, as no other language would express such depth of thought united with such ardent feeling. I rather apprehend that Marini, who is not a man of much education, was not competent to give effect to powerful emotion in any language: but the missionaries also declare that there is considerable difficulty in translating from the O Wahi language, which is particularly adapted to poetry.

Karemaku touched also on the change that had taken place in the religion of the country.—"Our present belief," said he, "is preferable to that which it has supplanted; but the inhabitants of the mountains cannot understand its superiority; and strong measures are necessary to prevent their relapsing into idolatry. The King should not have so suddenly annihilated all that they held sacred. As a first consequence, he has been obliged to seek for safety in a foreign country. How all will end, I cannot foresee; but I look forward with fear. The people are attached to me, and I have influence over them; but my health declines, and the Government, which I have scarcely been able to keep together, will probably not survive me. Blood will be spilt, and anarchy will prevail. Already the island of O

Tuai has revolted, even during my life." These fears are not without foundation: they are shared by the natives and the foreign settlers; and many of the Yeris seem persuaded that the monarchy will be dismembered on Karemaku's death. Some have already fixed upon the districts they mean to appropriate, and do not even take any pains to conceal their intentions. Yet has the aged and infirm Karemaku hitherto maintained order among these turbulent spirits, permitting no one to disturb the general tranquillity with impunity.

During my former visit here, the painter Choris, who made the voyage with me, and was afterwards murdered in Mexico, took an excellent likeness of Tameamea. I now presented to the venerable Karemaku a copper-plate engraving from this picture. The joy with which he received it was really affecting; he gazed on the picture with delight, and kissed it several times, while the tears rolled down his cheeks. On taking leave, he begged that he might have the medical assistance from our physician, as he had been long indisposed. He pressed my hand, saying, "I too am a Christian, and can read and write." That a warrior, and a statesman, should pride himself on such advantages as these above all others, proves the estimation in which they are held. The Sandwich Islanders know that these are the ties which connect them with civilized nations.

Karemaku and his wife were, notwithstanding the extreme heat, dressed entirely in the European fashion. He wore a dark surtout, and black waistcoat, and pantaloons, both of very fine cloth. He was still in mourning for his beloved Tameamea, and his hat was bound with crape. The lady's dress was of black silk. A crowd of people of both sexes assembled to welcome the Regent. His foot had scarcely touched the shore, when they all began to rub each other's noses, and at a given signal, to weep aloud. This is the established etiquette in welcoming a great chief. Some of the old women of rank surrounded Karemaku, under Chinau's direction, and rubbing each other's noses, sang in a plaintive tone a song to the following effect:

"Where hast thou stayed so long, beloved ruler? We have wept for thee every day. Heaven be praised that thou art here again! Dost thou feel how the earth rejoices under thy footsteps? Dost thou hear how the pigs which scent thee, joyfully grunt their welcome? Dost thou smell the roasted fish that waits thy eating? Come, we will cherish thee, that thou mayest take comfort among us." It must be confessed, that if the O Wahi language be peculiarly adapted for poetry, this composition does not do it justice. Karemaku laughed at this reception, and allowed himself to be conducted in grand procession to Nomahanna, who had not condescended to meet him. The excitement lasted the whole day. Nothing was spoken of but Karemaku's heroism, and the rebel son of Tamaris, whom he had brought with him a prisoner. This young man is called Prince George; he is about five-and-twenty, and not of a prepossessing appearance. He dresses like a European; but although educated in the United States of America, he scarcely equals a common sailor in moral attainments, and is remarkable only for his vices. Karemaku never loses sight of him. Two Yeris are appointed for his keepers; and he knows that he should be strangled if he attempted to escape.

Kahumanna still remained in O Tuai, to maintain the newly-restored tranquillity. This female, who had already distinguished herself in Vancouver's time, unites a clear understanding with a masculine spirit, and seems to have been born for dominion.

Karemaku's arrival proved extremely useful to us. We had made the disagreeable discovery that a great part of the copper with which the ship was bottomed had become loose, and the hull thereby liable to injury from worms. To repair this damage in the ordinary way, the laborious task of unlading and keel-hauling must have been undertaken; but our noble friend, on hearing of our difficulties, put us upon an easier method of managing the business. He sent me three very clever divers, who worked under the water, and fastened new plates of copper on the hull, two of them provided with hammers to drive in the nails, while the third held the materials. We found that these men could remain at work forty-eight seconds at a time. When they emerged, their eyes were always red and starting; the effect of the violent strain upon the optic nerve which the use of the sight under water produces. We had some skilful divers among our own sailors, who, although they could not have attempted this work, were able to inspect what was done by the Wahuaners, and to report that it was properly executed.

Some days after Karemaku's arrival, came an ambassador from Nomahanna, with instructions to demand an audience of me. I received him in the cabin. His only clothing, except a pocket of plaited reeds that hung round his neck, was a shirt, and a very broad-brimmed straw hat. The fellow looked important and mysterious, as if he had a mighty secret to impart; but converse with each other we could not, for he understood only his mother-tongue, of which I was entirely ignorant; he therefore informed me by signs that his pocket contained something for me, and drew from it a packet. One by one, a multitude of envelopes of the paper manufactory of the country were removed, till at length a letter came to light, which he handed to me with the words, "Aroha Nomahanna!" a salutation from Nomahanna. He then explained to me, in pantomime, that it was the Queen's intention to visit me to-day, and that she requested I would send my boat to fetch her. After saying a great deal about "Pala pala," he left me, and I summoned Marini, who gave me the following translation of the letter.

"I salute thee, Russian! I love thee with my whole heart, and more than myself. I feel, therefore, on seeing thee again in my country, a joy which our poor language is unequal to express. Thou wilt find all here much changed. While Tameamea lived, the country flourished; but since his death, all has gone to ruin. The young King is in London. Karemaku and Kahumanna are absent; and Chinau, who fills their place, has too little power over the people to receive thee as becomes thy rank. He cannot procure for thee as many hogs and sweet potatoes, and as much tarro as thou hast need of. How sincerely do I regret that my great possessions lie upon the Island of Muwe, so far away across the sea! Were they nearer, thou shouldst daily be surrounded by hogs. As soon as Karemaku and Kahumanna return, all thy wants shall be provided for. The King's brother comes with them; but he is yet only an inexperienced boy, and does not know how to distinguish good from evil.

"I beg thee to embrace thine Emperor in my name. Tell him, that I would willingly do so myself, but for the wide sea that lies between us. Do not forget to carry my salutations to thy whole nation. Since I am a Christian, and that thou art also such, thou wilt excuse my indifferent writing. Hunger compels me to close my letter. I wish that thou also mayst eat thy hog's head with appetite and pleasure.

I am,
With royal constancy
And endless love, thine,

NOMAHANNA."

This curious epistle is very neatly written in a firm hand. The letters are large, well-formed, and very intelligible. The superscription bears only the words with which the letter begins—"Aroha Rukkini!" The composition had taken her many weeks to complete; she made some progress in it every day; but what was once inserted she never altered; the same clean page that had been transmitted to me, being the identical one on which the letter was commenced.

It was soon known in Hanaruro that the Queen had written to me; and as all she did was imitated, I was presently in a fair way for being honoured with many similar letters. All my intended correspondents, however, would require at least as much time to express their thoughts on paper, as

Nomahanna had taken; I must therefore have waited for their favours much longer than would have been convenient.

According to Nomahanna's request, I sent off an officer with the shallop to fetch her: some hours, however, elapsed before she came, her Majesty's toilette having, said my officer, occupied all this time. When at length it was completed, she desired him to give her his arm and conduct her to the shallop. This is another imitation of European customs.

For a lady of the Sandwich Islands, Nomahanna was this day very elegantly attired. A peach-coloured dress of good silk, trimmed at the bottom with black lace, covered her Majesty's immense figure, which a very broad many-coloured sash, with a large bow in the front, divided exactly into two halves. She had a collar round her neck of native manufacture, made of beautiful red and yellow feathers; and on her head a very fine Leghorn hat, ornamented with artificial flowers from Canton, and trimmed round the edge with a pendant flounce of black lace; her chin lying modestly hidden behind a whole bed of flowers that bloomed on her mountain bosom. In somewhat striking contrast to all this finery were the clumsily accoutred feet, and stout, ill-shaped, brown, unstockinged legs, which the shortness of her Majesty's petticoats, proportioned originally to the stature of a European belle, displayed to a rather unsightly extent.

As yet, the shoemaker's craft does not flourish in the Sandwich Islands; so that all the shoes and boots worn there are imported from Europe and America. But as neither of these Continents can produce such a pair of feet as those of Queen Nomahanna, the attempt to force them into any ready-made shoes would be hopeless; and her Majesty is therefore obliged, if she would not go bare-foot, which she does not consider altogether decorous, to content herself with a pair of men's galloshes. Such trifles as these were, however, beneath her notice, and she contemplated her dress with infinite complacency, as a pattern of princely magnificence. In these splendid habiliments, with a parasol in her hand, slowly and with difficulty, she climbed the ship's stairs, on which, with some of my officers, I was in waiting to receive her; on the highest step she endeavoured already to give us a proof of her acquaintance with our customs, by making a courtesy, which was intended to accord with the most approved rules of the art of dancing, though the feet, not perfectly tutored in their parts, performed in rather a comic style. In attempting this feat, she lost her balance, and would have fallen into the water, if a couple of strong sailors had not caught her illustrious person in their arms.

She was much delighted with all that she saw on board, especially with my cabin, where the sofa paid dearly for the honour of her approbation,— she sat upon it, and broke it down. The portrait of the Emperor Alexander attracted her particular attention; she sat down opposite to it upon the floor, where she could cause no farther destruction, and said, after gazing upon it for some minutes with much interest, "Maitai, Yeri nue Rukkini!" (the great Governor of the Russians is beautiful!) She told me, that she knew a great deal about Russia. A Sandwich Islander, named Lauri, who, in 1819, had made the voyage thither, in the Russian ship Kamtschatka, with Captain Golowin, and had afterwards returned to his own country, had told her many things concerning Petersburg and the Emperor. She said she would have liked to make the voyage herself, but that Lauri's fearful description of the cold had terrified her. He had told her, that it was necessary to envelope the body entirely in fur, and that even this would not obviate all danger of losing the nose and ears; that the cold changed the water into a solid substance, resembling glass in appearance, but of so much strength that it was used for a high road, people passing over it in huge chests drawn by horses, without breaking it; that the houses were as high as mountains, and so large, that he had walked three days in one of them without coming to the end of it. It was evident that Lauri had stretched a little; but Nomahanna had no notion of incredulity. She approved of our inventions for warming the inside of our houses, and thought, that if she were at Petersburg, she would not go out at all during the cold weather, but would drive her carriage about the house. She inquired how it could possibly be so warm at one season of the year, and so cold at another. I endeavoured to accommodate my answer to her powers of comprehension, and she seemed satisfied.

"Lauri was in the right," she observed; "there are very clever people in Russia." Her acknowledgment of my abilities, however, proved rather inconvenient, for she now overwhelmed me with a host of questions, some of them very absurd, and which to have answered with methodical precision, would have required much time and consideration. For instance, she desired me to tell her how much wood must be burnt, every year, to warm all the countries of the earth? Whether rain enough might not fall, at some time or other, to extinguish all the fires? And whether, by means of such a rain, Wahu might not become as cold as Russia? I endeavoured to cut the matter as short as possible; and, in order to divert her thoughts to other subjects, set wine before her; she liked it very much, and I therefore presented her with a bottle; but her thirst for knowledge was not thus to be quenched, and during a visit of two hours, she asked such incessant questions, that I was not a little relieved when, at length, she proposed to depart. In taking leave, she observed, "If I have wine, I must have glasses, or how can I drink it?" So saying, she took the bottle that had been given her, in one hand, and, with the other, seizing without ceremony the glasses that stood on the table, she went upon deck. There she made a profound courtesy to all present, and again took her seat in the shallop. Thus ended this condescending visit, with the royal appropriation of my wine glasses. Nomahanna had, however, been so liberal to us, that she had a right to suppose she would be welcome to them.

The illness of Karemaku had very much increased since his arrival in Wahu; he had every symptom of dropsy. Our physician, however, succeeded, in a great measure, in restoring him to health, and when I paid him a congratulatory visit, I found him very grateful for the benefit he had received, full of spirits, and very facetious. I adopted his tone, and jestingly told him, that we would certainly complete his cure, even if we should be obliged to rip open his stomach, take out the bowels, clean them, and replace them. Karemaku laughed, and said he would submit to the operation, if it was necessary to his perfect recovery. Some old women, however, who were present, took the matter in sober seriousness, and spread among the people a report of the dreadful treatment their beloved Karemaku was threatened with; a terrible disturbance in Hanaruro was the consequence. The people believed I intended to kill him, and were excessively irritated against me. Karemaku himself sent me this intelligence through Marini; adding a request, that I would not come ashore again till he had overcome this foolish idea, which was accomplished in a few days. The feeling manifested on this occasion was certainly honourable both to the governor and the governed.

An epidemic disease prevailed this year throughout the Sandwich Islands. It produced a great mortality, death generally following the attack within a few days. In Hanaruro I saw many corpses daily carried to their burial; but nowhere is recovery from serious illness so improbable as here. As soon as the patient is obliged to take to his bed, he is immediately surrounded by his nearest relations, especially of the female sex, who, weeping, and singing mournful songs in a most lamentable tone, propose to themselves, by this means, to effect his recovery, or at least to procure him some relief from his sufferings. The worse he grows, the larger the assembly, and the louder the noise becomes; even his friends and acquaintances come flocking in: when there is no more room within the house, they congregate round the door, and continue mourning, crying, and howling, inside and outside, till the sufferer expires. This perpetual disturbance, the constant remembrance of death it occasions, and the infection of the air from the number of breaths in the crowded apartment, naturally produce a very prejudicial effect, and no doubt many die rather in consequence of these proofs of sympathy than of their disease.

Kahumanna, having concluded her business in O Tuai, arrived at length in Hanaruro with the King's brother, a handsome boy of thirteen. I paid her a visit, and was very graciously received. She is considerably older than Nomahanna; but, though large and corpulent enough, not by much such a prodigy of size. Her countenance bears traces of former beauty; she dresses entirely like a European, and has a more intimate knowledge of our customs and manners than Nomahanna. Her house, built partly of wood and partly of stone, is larger than the one I have described as the habitation of the other Queen; like that, it has two stories and a balcony, and it is similarly furnished. Near it is the abode of the missionary Bengham. Kahumanna, as well as Nomahanna, has the date of Tameamea's death marked upon her arm; otherwise they are not tattooed, which indeed few are, and those only the most aged people.

Kahumanna honoured me several times with visits on board, and condescended to write me a letter, which, Marini assured me, contained nothing but expressions so inflated and pompous that he could not understand, and therefore could not translate them.

The appointed time for our return to New Archangel now approached. Our vessel had been fully prepared for encountering the violent and continued storms of the North, and I waited the return of our mineralogist, M. Hoffman, who had gone to O Wahi, for the purpose of climbing the mountain Mou-na-roa, in which however he did not succeed. By command of Queen Nomahanna, assistance had indeed been afforded him; but the two Kanackas, who accompanied him as guides, refused to proceed farther than seven thousand feet above the level of the sea, or about half-way up the mountain; a height to which the most courageous O Wahian will scarcely venture, from fear partly of the spirits which haunt the summit of the mountain, partly of the cold, which is almost too severe for an inhabitant of the tropics to endure. At this point the Kanackas threw themselves flat upon the earth, nor would they stir another step, although certain of punishment for their refusal. In vain M. Hoffman tried to shake their resolution, first by offering them large presents, and then by threatening them with a loaded pistol; they were immoveable, and he was forced to return. His expedition, however, was not altogether fruitless: besides his mineralogical observations, he discovered an extraordinary cave, running at an acute angle several hundred feet deep into the mountain, where he found a sheet of water, which stretched as far as the light of the torches permitted the light to reach through the fearful darkness. It would have been interesting to have traversed this subterranean sea in a boat. It is most remarkable, that the water of this lake is salt, and that the alternate ebb and flow of the tide is as perceptible here as on the coast. M. Hoffman will probably publish other particulars respecting this natural curiosity.

On the 31st of January 1825, we left the harbour of Hanaruro, having the pleasure to be accompanied by our friend Karemaku, who, by the help of our physicians, felt himself well enough to venture thus far. He brought with him several double canoes, which, as there was no wind, towed the ship quite out of the harbour, and far enough to sea to obviate any danger from the reefs; Karemaku then took leave of us with the most cordial expressions of friendship, wishing us a prosperous voyage and a speedy return. On a signal from him, the fortress fired five guns, which salute we immediately returned. Karemaku waved his hat from his boat, and continuing his "Arohas" so long as we were within hearing, was rowed back to the harbour. A fresh wind at this moment springing up, we lost sight of the beautiful island where we had passed our time so agreeably, and prepared, with far less prospect of satisfaction, to encounter the wintry storms of the North. I chose the channel between the islands of Wahu and O Tuai, as the most convenient outlet into the open ocean, for ships going northward from Hanaruro. We passed through it on the following day, and sailed direct for New Archangel.

The reader will willingly spare me any particular description of this troublesome voyage: I must only mention that, on the 14th of February, in latitude 35° and 155° longitude, we sailed over a point where, according to the assertion of some whale-fishers in Wahu, an island lies; but though the horizon was perfectly clear, we could discover no sign of land. Our voyage proved safer and more expeditious than is usual at this season.

Our astronomical observations on the Sandwich Islands gave the following results:—

Latitude of Hanaruro	21° 17' 57"
Longitude	158° 00' 30"
Longitude of the Eastern point of the	
island Muwe	156° 13' 10"
Longitude of the Western point	156° 48' 11"
Latitude of one of the small islands	
East of Maratai, which are not	
given in Vancouver's map	21° 13' 30"
Longitude	156° 49' 12".

The account of our residence at New Archangel is contained in the tenth Chapter.

On our return voyage to Wahu, we had constantly fine weather, though but little wind, so that it was not till the 29th of August we found ourselves in latitude 34°, where we first, in a clear star-light night, saw the comet which was then visible in the neighbourhood of Aldebaran; it had a tail four degrees and a half long. On the 4th of September we sailed over a point, occupied in Arrowsmith's chart by the island Laxara, without perceiving the smallest trace of it; the existence therefore of this island, which is said to have been early discovered by the Spanish navigators, remains doubtful.

When we reached the tropic, a brisk trade-wind carried us quickly to the Sandwich Islands, and on the 12th of September we already saw the Mouna-roa quite clearly, at a distance of a hundred and twenty-four miles, rising high above the horizon. On the following morning, we again dropped anchor before the harbour of Hanaruro, after a sail of thirty-five days from New Archangel.

As I only intended to take in a supply of fresh provisions and water, and then continue my voyage without farther delay, I considered it unnecessary to run into the harbour, and remained in the roads, although the south-wind to which they are exposed is sometimes dangerous to ships riding there. This wind, however, blows only at certain seasons, and is always announced by an over-clouded sky, long enough to afford time for taking shelter or standing out to sea.

On the morning after our arrival, a remarkable phenomenon occurred, of which we were witnesses throughout its duration. While the heavens were quite clear, a thick, black cloud formed itself over the island, resting its lower verge on the summits of the mountains, the densest portion of the cloud hanging over the little town of Hanaruro. The wind was perfectly calm, till on a sudden a violent gust blew from the north-east, and at the same time a crashing noise proceeded from the cloud, as if many ships were firing their guns; the resemblance was so perfect, that we might have supposed we heard alternately the individual shots of the opposing broadsides. The concussion lasted some minutes; and when it ceased, two stones shot from the cloud into the street of Hanaruro, and from the violence of the fall broke into several pieces. The inhabitants collected the still warm fragments, and judging by these, the stones must have weighed full fifteen pounds each. They were grey inside, and were externally surrounded by a black burnt crust. On a chemical analysis, they appeared to resemble the meteoric stones which have fallen in many countries.

In the short period of our absence, some important events had taken place. My readers will remember that the King and Queen of the Sandwich Islands arrived safely in London, and were there treated with particular attention by the English Court; and that they both died in that country, having previously expressed their desire to be buried in their native land. This wish was fulfilled by the English Government. The bodies, having been embalmed, were laid in magnificent coffins decorated with gold, and Lord Byron was appointed to carry them and the royal suite, back to Wahu. When he arrived there, and the news of the deaths of the King and Queen transpired, it produced a great but varying sensation. Some of the people lamented the loss, but the greater number rejoiced to be relieved of a ruler in whom they had no confidence; our friend Karemaku seemed much grieved, possibly from old attachment to the royal family, or from patriotism, as he had hoped that the King's visit to England would have been very advantageous to him, and no one was at the moment qualified to assume the reins of government as his successor.

On the 11th of May, both coffins were carried in solemn procession to the church, the fortress and the English frigate firing their guns. The people cried and howled, as custom requires on these occasions, but all the while greatly admiring the magnificence of the coffins; some remarked that it must be a pleasure to die in England, where people were laid in such beautiful boxes. The following inscriptions in the English language were on the coffin-lids:

"Tameamea II., King of the Sandwich Islands, died in London on the 24th of July 1824, in the 28th year of his age. Respected be the memory of our beloved King Jolani."

(The King was sometimes known by this appellation.)

"Tamehamelu, Queen of the Sandwich Islands, died in London, on the 8th of July 1824, in the 22nd year of her age."

The funeral procession was arranged in the following order: Twelve Yeris, in the national costume, with beautiful coloured feather mantles and helmets, walked first; they were followed by a band of musicians playing the dead-march, and a company of soldiers from the frigate Blond. Then came the chaplain of the frigate, and with him the missionaries, immediately followed by the coffins in hearses, each drawn by forty Yeris. Directly behind the coffins came the heir to the throne, the brother of the King, a boy about thirteen, dressed in European uniform. Lord Byron, his officers, and the royal family, followed, the procession being closed by the people, who, attracted by the novelty of the spectacle, assembled in great multitudes. All wore crape as a sign of mourning, or, if they could not procure this, Tapa. In the church, which was entirely hung with black, the chaplain of the English frigate read the funeral-service, and the procession afterwards repaired, in the order above described, to a small stone chapel, where the coffins were deposited, and where they still remain.

Soon after the funeral, the new King was proclaimed by the title of Tameamea the Third, at the command of Karemaku, who retained the regency during the minority, in conjunction with the Queen Kahumanna. The regents were thus nominally the same; but Karemaku was too ill to take an active share in the government, and the missionary Bengham found means to obtain such an acendency over the imperious Kahumanna, and, through her, over the nation, that in the course of only seven months an entire change had taken place:—we might have imagined ourselves in a different country. Bengham had undertaken the education of the young monarch, and was keeping him under the strictest *surveillance*. He meddles in all the affairs of government, and makes Kahumanna, and even sometimes Karemaku, the instrument of his will; pays particular attention to commercial concerns, in which he appears to take great interest; and seems to have quite forgotten his original situation and the object of his residence in the islands, finding the avocations of a ruler more to his taste than those of a preacher. This would be excusable, if his talents were of a nature to contribute to the instruction and happiness of the people; if he understood the art of polishing the rough diamond, to which the uncorrupted Sandwich Islander may aptly be compared, so as to bring out its intrinsic value, and to increase its external splendour. But the fact is widely different; and one cannot see without deep regret the spiritual and temporal weal of a well-disposed people committed to the guidance of an unenlightened enthusiast, whose ill-directed and ill-arranged designs are inimical to their true and permanent interests.

Mr. Stewart, also a missionary, but more recently settled here than Bengham, is a judicious and well-informed man, and would remedy many of the evils incident to the present state of affairs; but Bengham, who has usurped the absolute control of the spiritual administration, will have every thing accommodated to his whims. Stewart therefore, finding himself unable to follow the course prescribed by his active zeal and strong understanding, for the benefit of the islanders, proposes to leave the country.

That Bengham's private views may not be too easily penetrated, religion is made the cloak of all his designs, and the greatest activity and strictness prevail in its propagation, and in the maintenance of church discipline. The inhabitants of every house or hut in Hanaruro are compelled by authority to an almost endless routine of prayers; and even the often dishonest intentions of the foreign settlers must be concealed under the veil of devotion. The streets, formerly so full of life and animation, are now deserted; games of all kinds, even the most innocent, are sternly prohibited; singing is a punishable offence; and the consummate profligacy of attempting to dance would certainly find no mercy. On Sundays, no cooking is permitted, nor must even a fire be kindled: nothing, in short, must be done; the whole day is devoted to prayer, with how much real piety may be easily imagined. Some of the royal attendants, on their return from London, at first opposed these regulations, and maintained that the English, though good Christians, submit to no such restraint. Kahumanna, however, infatuated by her counsellor, will hear of no opposition; and as her power extends to life and death, those who would willingly resist are compelled to bend under the iron sceptre of this arbitrary old woman.

A short time before our return, a command had issued, that all persons who had attained the age of eight years should be brought to Hanaruro, to be taught reading and writing. The poor country people, though much discontented, did not venture to disobey, but patiently abandoning their labour in the fields, flocked to Hanaruro, where we saw many families bivouacking in the streets, in little huts hastily put together, with the spelling-books in their hands. Such as could already read were made to learn passages from the Bible by heart. Every street in Hanaruro has more than one school-house: they are long huts, built of reeds, without any division. In each of these, about a hundred scholars, of both sexes, are instructed by a single native teacher, who, standing on a raised platform, names aloud every single letter, which is repeated in a scream by the whole assembly. These establishments, it may be supposed, are easily recognised afar off; no other sounds are heard in the streets; and the human figure is seldom to be seen amidst this melancholy stillness, except when the scholars, conducted by their teachers, repair to the church. Every sort of gaiety is forbidden.

Lord Byron had brought with him from England a variety of magic lanterns, puppet-shows, and such like toys, and was making preparations to exhibit them in public, for the entertainment of the people, when an order arrived from Bengham to prevent the representation, because it did not become God-fearing Christians to take pleasure in such vain amusements. The nobleman, not wishing to dispute the point, gave up his good-natured intentions.

That a people naturally so lively, should readily submit to such gloomy restrictions at the command of their rulers, proves how easily a wise government might introduce among them the blessings of rational civilization. Well might Karemaku exclaim, "Tameamea, thou hast died too soon!" Had this monarch doubled the usual age of man, and accorded his protection to such a reformer as Stewart, the Sandwich Islanders might by this time have acquired the respect of all other nations, instead of retrograding in the arts of civilization, and assuming under compulsion the hypocritical appearance of an affected devotion.

In taking a walk with an American merchant established here, I met a naked old man with a book in his hand, whom my companion addressed, and knowing him for a determined opponent of the new system, expressed his surprise at his occupation, and enquired how long he had been studying his alphabet. With a roguish laugh which seemed intended to conceal a more bitter feeling, first looking round to make sure that he should not be overheard, he replied, "Don't think that I am learning to read. I have only bought the book to look into it, that Kahumanna may think I am following the general example; she would not otherwise suffer me to approach her, and what would then become of a poor, miserable, old man like me? What is the use of the odious B A, Ba? Will it make our yams and potatoes grow? No such thing; our country people are obliged to neglect their fields for it, and scarcely half the land is tilled. What will be the consequence? There will be a famine by and by, and "Pala, Pala" will not fill a hungry man."

It is doubtless praiseworthy in a government to provide for the instruction of the people, but to force it upon them by such unreasonable measures as those adopted by Kahumanna and her counsellor must have a prejudicial effect: so far the old man was right.

A striking instance of the severity with which the Queen sometimes prosecutes her purpose, fell under our observation. An old man of seventy, who rented a piece of land belonging to her, many miles distant from Hanaruro, had always paid his taxes with regularity, and hoping that the distance, and his advanced age, might dispense with his attendance at the church and the school, acted accordingly; but for this neglect, Kahumanna drove him from his home. He sought her presence, implored her compassion for his destitute condition, and represented the impossibility of learning to read at his age. But in vain! The Queen replied with an angry gesture, "If you will not learn to read, you may go and drown yourself."

To such tyranny as this, has Bengham urged the Queen, and perhaps already esteems himself absolute sovereign of these islands. But he reckons without his host. He pulls the cord so tightly, that the bow must break; and I forewarn him, that his authority will, one day, suddenly vanish: already the cloud is gathering; much discontent exists. The injudicious summons of country people to Hanaruro has enhanced the price of provisions, partly on account of the increased consumption, partly because so much time spent in study and prayer leaves but little for the labours of agriculture. Thus will the approaching pressure of want be added to the slavery of the mind, and probably urge the islanders to burst their fetters. I have myself heard many of the Yeris express their displeasure, and the country people, who consider Bengham's religion as the source of all their sufferings, one night set fire to the church: the damage sustained was trifling, and the flames were soon extinguished; but the incendiaries were not discovered.

Karemaku is suffering under a confirmed dropsy. Lord Byron's surgeon tapped him; but, by the time we arrived, the increase of his disorder required a repetition of the operation; it was performed with great success by our surgeon. But it is impossible he can survive long, and his death will be the signal of a general insurrection, which Bengham's folly will certainly have accelerated.

Our second visit to Hanaruro was as disagreeable as the first had been pleasant: even our best friend, Nomahanna, was quite altered, and received us with coldness and taciturnity, we therefore laid in our stock of provisions and fresh water as quickly as possible, and rejoiced in being at liberty to take leave of a country from whence one wrong-headed man has banished cheerfulness and content.

Several whalers were lying in the harbour, and among them the Englishman we had met with in St. Francisco, and who had then been so unsuccessful. Fortune had since been more propitious to him, and he was now returning from the coast of Japan with a rich cargo of spermaceti valued at twenty-five thousand pounds sterling: he had touched here to take in provisions for his voyage homewards.

I learnt from another captain the particulars of an accident that had happened to one of his companions, which shows the dangers whale-fishers are exposed to, and is a singular example of a providential escape.

A North American, Captain Smith, sailed in the year 1820 in a three-masted ship, the Albatross, for the South Sea, in pursuit of the spermaceti whale. When nearly under the Line, west of Washington's Island, they perceived a whale of an extraordinary size. The boats were all immediately lowered, and, to make the capture more sure, they were manned with the whole crew: the cook's mate alone remained at the helm, and the ship lay-to. The monster, as it peaceably floated on the surface of the water, was eagerly followed, and harpooned. On feeling the stroke of the weapon, it lashed its powerful tail with fury, and the boat nearest it was obliged to dart with all speed out of the way, to avoid instant destruction. The whale then turned its vengeance on the ship, swam several times round her with prodigious noise, and then struck her so violently on the bows, that the cook's mate could compare the effect of the blow only to the shock of an earthquake. The fish disappeared, but the tremendous leak the ship had sprung sank her in five minutes with all that she contained. Her solitary guardian was with difficulty saved.

The crew were now left in four open boats, several weeks' voyage from the nearest land, and with no provision but the little biscuit they happened to have with them. After a long discussion upon the best course to pursue, they separated: two of the boats steered for the Washington or Marquesas

Isles; and the other two, with the Captain in one of them, towards the south, for the island of Juan Fernandez. The former have not since been heard of; but the latter were, a fortnight afterwards, picked up by a vessel, when the captain and four only of his men were found alive: the other ten had died of hunger, and their corpses had afforded nourishment to the survivors.

On the 19th of September, when the first rays of the sun were gilding the romantic mountains of Wahu, we spread our sails, and bade adieu to the Sandwich Islands, heartily wishing them what they so greatly want—another Tameamea, not in name only, but in spirit and in deed.

THE PESCADORES, THE RIMSKI-KORSAKOFF, THE ESCHSCHOLTZ, AND THE BRONUS ISLES

ON leaving the Sandwich Isles, we steered southward, it being my intention to sail by a track not hitherto pursued by navigators who have left us records of their voyages, to the Radack chain of islands. At Hanaruro, several captains had mentioned to me an island situated in 17° 32' latitude, and 163° 52' longitude. On the 23rd of September we crossed this point, and saw indeed birds of a description that rarely fly to any great distance from land; but the reported island itself we were unable to descry even from the mast-head, although the atmosphere was perfectly clear:—so little is the intelligence of masters of trading-vessels to be relied on.

On the 26th, we were, by observation, in 14° 32' latitude, and 169° 38' longitude. During the whole of the day, large flights of such sea-birds were seen as indicate the neighbourhood of land, and even some land-birds; so that no doubt remained of our having sailed at no great distance from an island hitherto unknown, the discovery of which is reserved for some future voyager. During the whole of this course, we had frequent signs of the vicinity of land, but never to the same extent as on this day.

A captain, who had frequently made the voyage from the Sandwich Isles to Canton, asserts his having discovered a shoal in 14° 42' latitude, and 170° 30' longitude. I can neither confirm nor confute this assertion; and my only motive for repeating it here is, that vessels passing near that point may be put upon their guard.

On the 5th of October we reached the Udirik group, the most northern of the islands belonging to the Radack chain. We sailed past its southern point, at a distance of only three miles, for the purpose of rectifying our longitude, that, in case of discovering the Ralik chain, we might be enabled to ascertain the exact difference between that and Radack. We therefore continued our course due west, in the direction of the Pescadore Islands, to obtain ocular demonstration that these and the Udirik group are not one and the same; an opinion which is still entertained by some persons, on the ground that the discoverers of the former have mistaken their longitude.

We continued our course due west throughout the day, with very fine weather, and having a man constantly upon the look-out from the mast-head. During the night we had the benefit of the full moon; we then carried but little sail; but at break of day we again set all our top-sails.

At noon, the watch called from the tops that land was right ahead of us. It soon came in sight, and proved to be a group of low, thickly-wooded coral islands, forming, as usual, a circle round a basin. At one o'clock in the afternoon we reached within three miles of them, and had, from the mast-head, a clear view of their whole extent. While occupied in surveying them, we doubled their most southern point, at a distance of only half a mile from the reefs, and perceived that their greatest length is from east to west, in which direction they take in a space of ten miles. The aspect of these green islands is pleasing to the eye, and, according to appearance, they would amply supply the necessities of a population not superabundant; but though we sailed very near them, and used our telescopes, we could discover no trace of human habitation.

According to accurate astronomical observations, the middle of this group lies under 11° 19' 21" latitude, and 192° 25' 3" longitude. In comparing the situation of the Pescadores, as given by Captain Wallis, their discoverer, with this observation, it is scarcely possible to believe in the identity of the groups. I have, however, left them the name of Pescadores, because the two observations nearly correspond. After having sailed round the whole group, we came, at four o'clock in the afternoon, so close to their north-western point, that every movement on land might have been distinctly seen with the naked eye; yet even here there was nothing to indicate the presence of man, though Wallis communicated with the inhabitants, if, indeed, these islands be really the Pescadores. If so, these people must have become extinct long ago, as no monument of their former existence is now visible. When we had completed our survey, we again proceeded westward, and, within half an hour, the watch again announced land in sight. The evening was now so far advanced, that we determined to lay-to, in order to avoid the danger of too near an approach to the coral reefs during the night, and deferred our survey till the following morning. At break of day we saw the islands which we have called the Pescadores, lying six miles to the eastward; whilst those which had risen on our horizon the preceding evening had wholly disappeared. We had diverged from them in the night; but, with a brisk trade-wind, we regained the sight of them in an hour. At eight o'clock in the morning we came within three miles of the nearest island, and running parallel with the land, began our examination. It was another group of coral islands connected by reefs round a basin. Here also vegetation was luxuriant, and the cocoa-trees rose to a towering height, but not a trace of man could be discerned; and we therefore concluded they were uninhabited, as we were near enough to distinguish any object with the naked eye. Favoured by a fresh breeze, we sailed westward along the islands, till nightfall, without reaching the end of this long group. During the night we had much difficulty in keeping our position, owing to a tolerably smart gale, which, in these unknown waters, would have been attended by no inconsiderable danger, but that the land lay to windward of us; and were therefore well pleased in the morning to find that the different landmarks by which we had been guided overnight, were still visible, so that we were enabled to pursue our observations without interruption.

The greatest length of this group, which I named, after our second lieutenant, Rimski-Korsakoff, is from east-north-east to west-south-west, in which direction it is, fifty-four miles long. Its greatest breadth is ten miles. As we were sailing along the islands to windward of us, we could plainly distinguish from the mast-head those which lay at the other side of the basin.

After having terminated our observations, we pursued a southerly course, in hopes of discovering more land, and sailed at a great rate during the whole of the day, without seeing any thing. At night we lay-to; but the following morning, the 9th of October, we had scarcely spread our sails, before the man at the mast-head discovered some low islands to the north, which we had already past, and which now lay to windward of us. I immediately changed our course, and endeavoured to approach them by dint of tacking, but a strong easterly current, which increased as we drew nearer to the land, almost baffled our efforts. We succeeded with much difficulty in getting within eleven miles and a half of the western extremity of the group, distinguished by a small round hill, which at noon lay due east, our latitude by observation being 11° 30' 32", and our longitude 194° 34'. From this point we could see the group, stretching to the verge of the horizon, in a south-easterly and north-easterly direction. We again attempted to approach them nearer; but not succeeding, we were obliged to continue our course to the westward, contenting ourselves with determining the position of the western extremity, 11° 40' 11" latitude, and 194° 37' 35" longitude, from which point they must stretch considerably to the east. These, like other coral islands, probably lie round a basin: of population we could see no trace, though there was every appearance of their being habitable. I named them, after our worthy Doctor and Professor, Eschscholtz, who was now making the second voyage with me.

It is unnecessary to add any thing here respecting the situations of these three groups of isles, which have been laid down, with the greatest possible accuracy, in the chart accompanying this volume; one thing only I beg to observe, that they bear not the slightest resemblance to the Pescadores described by Wallis. He did not possess the facilities for ascertaining the longitude, which have been invented since his time. His Pescadores may be situated elsewhere; but even if one of these groups should be the Pescadores, we may justly claim the discovery of the other two. This discovery is of some value, inasmuch as these groups are no doubt the northern extremity of the Ralik chain; and their position and distance from Radak being now ascertained, there will hereafter be little difficulty in discovering the remaining groups of the chain.

From the Eschscholtz Isles we steered for the Bronus Isles, it being my wish to try the accuracy of their geographical position, and to ascertain whether the interval between the two groups was wholly free of islands. On the 11th of October, at noon, being in latitude 11° 21' 39", and longitude 196° 35', the Bronus Isles were descried from the mast-head, at a distance of twenty miles. We approached within a mile and a half of the southern extremity of the group, from which point we were able to survey the whole, which we found, like other coral groups, to consist of a circle of islands connected by a reef. The Bronus Isles, however, appeared of more ancient formation than any we had yet seen; the land was somewhat more elevated, and the trees were larger and stronger. Here also we saw no appearance of inhabitants.

A calm which suddenly set in exposed us to the danger of being driven by a powerful current upon the reef; but when we were already very near the breakers, the direction of the current varied, running southward parallel with the coast. By this means we were enabled to double the southern extremity of the group, and a gentle breeze soon after springing up, conveyed us to a safe distance from the land. According to our observation, this southern extremity lies in latitude 11° 20' 50", and longitude 197° 28' 30". It was my intention to have noted the position of the whole group, for which purpose I endeavoured during the night to keep the ship in its vicinity; but at daybreak the current had carried us so far to leeward, that land could scarcely be perceived from the mast-head. As it was utterly impossible to make any way against the united force of the current and trade-wind, I was obliged to abandon my design, upon which we steered for the Ladrones, or Mariana Isles, where I intended to take in fresh provisions.

It is a striking phenomenon, and one not easily accounted for, that in 11° north latitude, from the Radak chain to the Bronus Isles, there should be a current of a mile and a half per hour.

THE LADRONES, AND THE PHILIPPINE ISLANDS

HAVING, in my former voyage, given a detailed account of these islands, I need not here add much concerning them. A fresh breeze, and fine weather, made our voyage agreeable and rapid. On the morning of the 25th of October, we saw the island Sarpani, which belongs to the Ladrones, lying before us at the distance of twenty-five miles, and soon after distinguished the principal island, Guaham, whither we were bound. The longitude of the eastern point of Sarpani was found to be 214° 38'.

The aspect of the eastern point of Guaham, which is exposed to a constant trade-wind, does not suggest an idea of the fertility of the island; but the traveller is agreeably surprised at the sight of its western coast, where Nature has been most prodigal; and cannot but remember with sorrow the extermination of the natives by the Spaniards, on their taking possession of the islands and forcibly introducing the Catholic religion.

It is remarkable that the soil of Guaham, under the first stratum of earth, consists of coral blocks not yet quite dissolved; from which it may be conjectured, that a former group of low coral islands, as well as the basin which they enclosed, were forced upwards by the power of subterranean fire; and in this manner the island of Guaham has been formed. This hypothesis is confirmed by Mr. Hoffman's discovery of a crater on the island, with a fire still burning in its abyss.

The fortress, standing on what is called the Devil's Point, intended for the defence of the town of Agadna, was so peacefully disposed, that not one of its cannons was fit for use. I saw, to my great astonishment, in the harbour Caldera de Apra, ships bearing the English and North American flags. The Spaniards do not usually permit the entrance of foreign vessels; but I was informed by the captains of these, that the whalers who pursue their occupations on the coast of Japan, now frequently choose Guaham for refitting and victualling their ships. I also heard, with much pleasure, that they exclusively use our Admiral Krusenstern's chart of the Japanese coast; and they assured me, that objects even of minor importance are laid down in it with the greatest accuracy. How much cause have seamen for thankfulness to one who has provided them with such a chart! their lives frequently depend on the correctness of these guides; and an erroneous one may be worse than none at all.

As I only intended stopping here a few days, and the harbour is by no means safe, I determined not to enter it, but sent an officer to the

Governor, with a list of fresh provisions which I requested his assistance in procuring. On the following morning, I rowed with some of my officers ashore, and we were received by the Governor, Don Gango Errero, who had already taken measures for supplying our wants, with great civility, though not without some degree of Spanish stateliness.

His government here confirms an observation repeatedly made, that a few years of a bad administration are sufficient to undo all that a good one may have effected by a long series of exertions. Eight years ago, when Medenilla was governor, the most perfect content, and prosperity to a certain extent, existed in Guaham; and now, by the fault of one man, every thing bears a totally different aspect. So much depends on the choice of the person to whom power is delegated, at such a distance from the seat of sovereignty as that the complaints of the oppressed can seldom reach it. Errero is even accused of the murder of some English and American sailors; and, on this occasion, Spanish justice has not been in vain appealed to by their comrades; for, as I afterwards learned, the order for Errero's arrest was already made out at the moment when, in perfect self-confidence and enjoyment, he was entertaining me with lively songs, accompanied by himself on the guitar; and Medenilla has been again appointed to the command, that he may endeavour to repair the evils Errero had occasioned.

Of my earlier acquaintances, I now met only the estimable Don Louis de Torres, the friend of the Carolinas, who communicated to M. De Chamisso many interesting particulars respecting these amiable islanders. After our departure in the Rurik, he had again made a voyage to the Carolinas, and had persuaded several families to come and settle at Guaham. The yearly visits of these islanders to Guaham are still regularly continued; and at the time of our stay, one of their little flotillas was in the harbour. Being clever seamen, they are much employed by the Spaniards, who are very ignorant in this respect, in their voyages to the other Marian Islands, with which, unassisted by their friends of Carolina, these would hold but little communication. We had an opportunity of seeing two of their canoes come in from Sarpani, when the sea ran high, and the wind was very strong, and greatly admired the skill with which they were managed.

The revolt of the Spanish colonies has not extended itself to these islands. The inhabitants of Guaham have maintained their loyalty, notwithstanding the tyranny of their governor, and unseduced by an example recently given them. A Spanish ship of the line and a frigate, with fugitive loyalists from Peru, lately touched here; they were bound for Manilla; but the crews of both ships mutinied, put the officers and passengers ashore, and returned to Peru to make common cause with the insurgents.

After remaining four days before Agadna, we took in our provisions, for which ten times the price was demanded that we had paid here eight years ago, and left Guaham on the 22nd of October, directing our course for the Bashi Islands, as I intended to pass through their straits into the Chinese Sea, and then sail direct to Manilla. On the 1st of November, our noon observation gave 20° 15' latitude, and 236° 42' longitude, so that we were already in the neighbourhood of the Bashi and Babuyan Islands. We continued to sail so briskly till sunset, that we could not be then far from land; but black clouds had gathered over it, concealing it from our view, and presaging stormy weather; we did not venture therefore to advance during the night, but tacked with sails reefed, waiting the break of day. At midnight we had some violent squalls from the north with a ruffled sea, but not amounting to a storm. The rising sun discovered to us the three high Richmond rocks, rising in the middle of the strait, between the Bashi and Babuyan Islands. Soon after the island of Bantan appeared, with heavy clouds still lingering behind its cliffs. The weather was, however, at present fine, the wind blowing strongly from the north; we therefore set as much sail as the gale would permit us to carry, and pursued our course through the strait formed by the Richmond rocks, and the southern Bashi Islands. In clearing these straits, we had reason to apprehend serious damage to our rigging, or even the loss of a mast. A heavy squall from the north-east put the sea in great commotion. The billows chafed and roared as they broke over each other, and were met in the narrow channel by a current, driving from the Chinese Sea into the ocean. This furious encounter of the contending waves produced the appearance of breakers, through which we were compelled to work our dangerous way; the ship, sometimes tossed to their utmost summit, then, without the power of resistance, suddenly precipitated into the yawning gulf between them, wore, however, through all her trials, and gave me cause for exultation in the strength of her masts, and the goodness of her tackling. We passed two hours in this anxious and critical condition, but at length emerged into the Chinese Sea; where the comparative peacefulness of the waves allowed us to repose after our fatigues, and even afforded us an opportunity of ascertaining our longitudes.

We found the longitude of the most

| easterly of the Richmond rocks | 237° 50' 2" |
| most westerly | 237° 52' 0" |

the eastern point	
of the Island of Bantan	237° 55' 32"
the western point	
of Babuyan	238° 00' 56"
the western point	
of the Bashi Island	238° 4' 47"
latitude of the eastern point	20° 15' 47".

All these longitudes are determined according to our chronometers, which were tried immediately after our arrival in Manilla. They differ from those on Horsbourg's new chart by three minutes and a half, ours being so much more westerly.

With a favourable wind we now sailed southwards, in sight of the western coast of Luçon, till we reached the promontory of Bajador, where we were detained some days by calms, therefore did not come in sight of Manilla bay till the 7th of November. Here the wind was violent and contrary; but as it blew from the land, could not materially swell the waves: we were therefore enabled, by tacking, to advance considerably forward; and at length contrived to run into the bay, by the southern entrance, between its shores and the island of Corregidor. A Spanish brig, which was tacking at the same time, lost both her top-masts in a sudden gust.

On the morning of the 8th of November we anchored before the town of Manilla. I immediately waited on Don Mariano Ricofort, the Governor of the Philippines. He gave me a friendly reception, and granted the permission I requested, to sail to Cavite, a hamlet lying on the bay, within a few miles of the town, and possessing the advantage of a convenient dock. Our ship being greatly in want of repair, we removed thither on the following day, and immediately commenced our labours.

We spent our time very pleasantly in this lovely tropical country. How richly has Nature endowed it, and how little is her bounty appreciated by the Spaniards! The whole world does not offer a more advantageous station for commerce than the town of Manilla, situated as it is in the neighbourhood of the richest countries of Asia, and almost midway between Europe and America. Spanish jealousy had formerly closed her port; but since the revolt of the American colonies, it has been opened to all nations, and the Philippines are consequently rising rapidly to importance. As yet, their export trade has been chiefly confined to sugar and indigo for Europe, and the costly Indian bird's-nest, and *Trepangs*, for China. The latter is a kind of sea-snail without a shell, which not only here, but on the Ladrones, Carolinas, and Pelew Islands, even as far as New Holland, is as eagerly sought after as the sea-otter on the north-west coast of America. The luxurious Chinese consider them a powerful restorative of strength, and purchase them as such at an exorbitant price. But what an inexhaustible store of commercial articles might not these islands export! Coffee of the best quality, cocoa, and two sorts of cotton, the one remarkably fine, the produce of a shrub, the other of a tree, all grow wild here, and with very little cultivation might be made to yield a prodigious increase of wealth. These productions of Nature are, however, so much neglected, that at present no regular trade is carried on in them. A great abundance of the finest sago trees, and whole woods of cinnamon, grow wild and unnoticed in Luçon. Nutmegs, cloves, and all the produce of the Moluccas, are also indigenous on these islands, and industry only (a commodity which, unfortunately, does not flourish here,) is wanting to make them a copious source of revenue. Pearls, amber, and cochineal, abound in the Philippines; and the bosom of the earth contains gold, silver, and other metals. For centuries past, have the Spaniards suffered all these treasures to lie neglected, and are even now sending out gold to maintain their establishments.

The regular troops here, as well as the militia, are natives. The officers are Spaniards, though many of them are born here, and all, at least with few exceptions, are extremely ignorant. It is said that the soldiers are brave, especially when blessed, and encouraged by the priests. As far, however, as I have had an opportunity of observing the military force, I cannot think it would ever make a stand against an European army. Not only are the troops badly armed, but even the officers, who are in fact distinguished from the privates only by their uniforms, have no idea of discipline; any sort of precision in their manœuvres is out of the question; and to find a sentinel comfortably asleep with his musket on his shoulder, is by no means an uncommon occurrence.

I was told that Luçon contained eight thousand regular troops, and that by summoning the militia, twenty thousand could be assembled.

The field of honour where the heroes of Luçon distinguish themselves is on the southern Philippine Islands, which are not yet subdued; they are inhabited by Mahommedan Indians, who are constantly at war with the Spaniards, and who, ranging as pirates over all the coasts inhabited by Christians, spread terror and desolation wherever they appear. From time to time some well manned gun-boats are sent in pursuit of these robbers; which expend plenty of ammunition with very little effect.

It is said that six thousand Chinese inhabit the suburbs of Manilla, to which they are restricted. The greater part of them are clever and industrious mechanics; the rest are merchants, and some of them very rich: they are the Jews of Luçon, but even more given to cheating and all kinds of meanness than are the Israelites, and with fewer, or rather with no exceptions. They enjoy no privileges above the lowest of the people, but are despised, oppressed, and often unjustly treated. Their covetousness induces them to submit to all this; and as they are entirely divested of any feeling of honour, a small profit will console them for a great insult. The yearly tax paid by every Chinese for liberty to breathe the air in Manilla, is six piastres; and if he wishes to carry on any sort of trade, five more; while the native Indian pays no more than five reals.

The Philippines also did not follow the example of the American colonies; for some disturbances among the Indians here, were not directed against the government, and an insurrection soon after attempted proved unsuccessful. The former were occasioned by a few innocent botanists wandering through the island in search of plants; and an epidemic disease breaking out among the Indians about the same time, of which many died, a report suddenly spread among them, that the foreign collectors of plants had poisoned the springs in order to exterminate them. Enraged at this idea, they assembled in great numbers, murdered several strangers, and even plundered and destroyed the houses of some of the old settlers in the town of Manilla. It has been supposed that the Spaniards themselves really excited these riots, that they might fish in the troubled waters.

The late governor, Fulgeros, is accused of not having adopted measures sufficiently active for repressing the insurrection. This judicious and amiable man, who was perhaps too mild a governor for so rude a people, was murdered in his bed a year after by a native, of Spanish blood, an officer in one of the regiments here, who followed up this crime by heading a mutiny of the troops. The insurgents assembled in the market-place, but were soon dispersed by a regiment which remained faithful, and in a few hours peace was re-established, and has not since been disturbed. The present governor, Ricofort, was sent out to succeed the unfortunate Fulgeros.

The King, affected by the loyalty displayed by the town of Manilla, at a time when the other colonies had thrown off their allegiance, presented it with a portrait of himself, in token of his especial favour. The picture was brought out by the new governor, and received with a degree of veneration which satisfactorily evinced the high value set by the faithful colony on the royal present. It was first deposited in a house in the suburb belonging to the Crown, and then made its entry into the town in grand procession, and was carried to the station of honour appointed for it in the castle. This important ceremony took place during our residence here, on the 6th of December; and three days previously, the King in effigy had held a court in the suburb. The house was splendidly illuminated: in front of it stood a piquet of well-dressed soldiers; sentinels were placed at all the doors; the apartments were filled with attendants, pages, and officers of every rank in gala uniforms; and the etiquette of the Spanish court was as much as possible adhered to throughout the proceedings. Persons whose rank entitled them to the honour of a presentation to the King, were conducted into the audience-chamber, which was splendidly adorned with hangings of Chinese silk: here the picture, concealed by a silk curtain, was placed on a platform raised a few steps from the floor, under a canopy of silk overhanging two gilded pillars. The colonel on duty acting as Lord Chamberlain, conducted the person to be presented before the picture, and raised the curtain. The King then appeared in a mantle lined with ermine, and with a crown upon his head; the honoured individual made a low bow; the King looked in gracious silence upon him; the curtain was again lowered, and the audience closed.

On the 6th of December, the immense multitudes that had assembled from the different provinces, to celebrate the solemn entry of the portrait into the capital of the islands, were in motion at daybreak. The lower classes were seen in all kinds of singular costumes, some of them most laughable caricatures, and some even wearing masks. Rockets and Chinese fireworks saluted the rising sun, producing of course, by daylight, no other effects than noise, smoke, and confusion, while elegant equipages rolled along the streets, scarcely able to make their way through the crowd. At nine o'clock, a royal salute thundered from the cannon of the fortress; and at twelve the procession began to move, displaying a rather ludicrous mixture of Spanish and Asiatic taste. I saw it from the windows of a house on its route, which commanded a very extensive view of the line of march. The cortège was led by the Chinese. First came a body of twenty-four musicians, some striking with sticks upon large round plates of copper, producing an effect not unlike the jingling of bells, and others performing most execrably upon instruments resembling clarionets. The sound of the copper plates was too confused to allow us to distinguish either time or tune—points of no great consequence perhaps; the choir, at least, did not trouble much about them. The musicians were followed by a troop of Chinese bearing silken banners, upon which were represented their idols, and dragons of all sorts and sizes, surrounded by hieroglyphical devices. Next followed, in a kind of litter richly ornamented, a young Chinese girl with a pair of scales in her hand, and intended, as I was told, to represent Justice, a virtue for which her country-people, in these parts, have not much cause to applaud themselves. Another set of musicians surrounded the goddess, making din enough with their copper plates to drown every complaint that might endeavour to reach her ear. Then came the rest of the Chinese, in different bands, with the symbols of their respective trades represented upon banners. Four Bacchantes, somewhat advanced in age, and in an attire more loose than was consistent with modesty, followed next: from their long, black, dishevelled hair, they might have been taken for Furies; and it was only their crowns of vine-leaves, and the goblets in their hands, that enabled us to guess what they were intended to represent. Bacchus, very much resembling a Harlequin, followed with his tambourine; and after him, a body of very immodest dancers: these, as the procession moved but slowly, halting frequently, had abundant opportunities of displaying their shameless talent, for the benefit of the shouting rabble. Why the procession should be disgraced by such an exhibition, it was not easy to conceive; but there were many other inconceivable matters connected with it. A troop of Indians followed, in motley and grotesque attire, intended to represent savages: they were armed with spears and shields, and kept up a continual skirmish as they marched. Next in procession was a battalion of infantry, composed of boys armed with wooden muskets and pasteboard cartridge-boxes, and followed by a squadron of hussars, also boys, with drawn sabres of wood, not riding, but carrying pasteboard horses: each of these had a hole cut in its saddle, through which the hussar thrust his feet, relieving the charger from any actual necessity of making use of his own—though, to show its high blood and mettlesome quality, each emulated his fellow in prancing, rearing, and kicking with front and hind-legs, to the no small danger of discomfiting the parade order of the squadron. To this redoubtable army succeeded a party of giants two fathoms high, dressed in the very extremity of fashion, the upper part of their bodies being represented in pasteboard, accompanied by ladies elegantly attired, and of nearly equal dimensions, and by some very small dwarfs: the business of this whole group was to entertain the populace with pantomimic gestures, and comic dances. Next came all sorts of animals, lions, bears, oxen, &c. of a size sufficiently gigantic to conceal a man in each leg. Then, with grave and dignified deportment, marched Don Quixote and his faithful Sancho. To the question, what the honourable Knight of the Rueful Countenance was doing there, somebody replied that he represented the inhabitants of Manilla, who were just then mistaking a windmill for a giant. The hero of Cervantes was followed by a body of military, seemingly marching under his command; and after them came two hundred young girls from the different provinces of the Philippine Islands, richly and tastefully attired in their various local costumes. Fifty of these young graces drew the triumphal car, richly gilt, and hung with scarlet velvet, which contained the picture of Ferdinand. Not content with the mantle the painter had given him, they had hung round him a real mantle of purple velvet embroidered with gold. By his side, and seated on a globe, was a tall female form dressed in white, with an open book in one hand, and in the other a wand, pointing towards the portrait. This figure was to represent the Muse of History:—may she one day cast a glance of friendly retrospection on the prototype of her pictured companion! A body of cavalry followed the car, and the carriages of the most distinguished inhabitants of the place closed the procession. Several Chinese triumphal arches crossed the streets, through which the retinue passed; they were temporary erections of wood, occupying the whole breadth of the street, and were decorated in the gayest and most showy manner by the Chinese, who, on this occasion, seemed to have spared no expense in order to flatter the vanity of the Spaniards.

When the royal effigy entered the town, it was received by the Governor and the whole clergy of Manilla, and the young girls were superseded by the townspeople, who had now the honour to draw the car amidst the incessant cry of "*Viva el Rey Fernando!*" The cannon thundered from the ramparts; the military bands played airs of triumph; and the troops, which were ranged in two files from the gate of the town to the church, presented arms, and joined their "Vivas" to those of the populace. The procession halted at the church; and the picture being carried in, the bishop performed the service; after which, the King was replaced on his car, and conducted to the residence of the Governor, where, at length, he was installed in peace.

Three days longer the rejoicings continued: bells were rung, guns were fired, and each evening the town and suburbs were magnificently illuminated: many houses exhibiting allegorical transparencies which occupied their whole front. But the illumination of the Chinese triumphal arches in the suburbs surpassed all the show: the dragons which ornamented them spat fire; flames of various colours played around them; and large fire-balls discharged from them emulated the moon in the heavens, till, from their increasing height, they seemed to disappear among the stars. Each of these edifices was of three stories, surrounded by galleries, on which, during the day, the Chinese performed various feats for the amusement of the people: there were conjurors, rope-dancers, magic lanterns, and even dramatic representations, the multitude eagerly flocking to the sight, and expressing their satisfaction in loud huzzas! I saw a tragedy performed on one of these galleries, in which a fat Mandarin, exhibiting a comic variety of grimaces and strange capers which would have done credit to Punchinello, submitted to strangulation at the command of his sovereign. At night, the people went about the streets masked, and letting off sky-rockets and Chinese fireworks. In several parts of the town, various kinds of spectacles were exhibited for the popular amusement: the air resounded with music, and public balls were gratuitously given.

This unexampled rejoicing for the reception of a testimonial of royal approbation, seems sufficiently to prove the loyalty of the Philippines, and the little probability of their revolting, especially if the mother-country does not show herself wholly a stepmother to her dutiful children.

On the 10th of January our frigate was ready to sail, and we left Manilla, the whole crew being in perfect health.

ST. HELENA

A FRESH north-east monsoon expedited our voyage, and we cut the equator on the 21st of January, in the longitude 253° 38'; then passing between the islands of Sumatra and Java, we reached the ocean, after having safely traversed the Chinese Sea from its northern to its southern boundary, and directed our course towards the Cape of Good Hope, where we intended staying to refresh. When we had reached to longitude 256°, 12° south latitude, the east wind, contrary to all rules at this season, changed for a westerly one, and blew a strong gale; the sky was covered with black clouds, and the rain fell in torrents. At midnight, while the storm was still raging, and the darkness complete, we witnessed the phenomenon known by the name of Castor and Pollux, and which originates in the electricity of the atmosphere; these were two bright balls of the size which the planet Venus appears to us, and of the same clear light; we saw them at two distinct periods, which followed quickly upon each other in the same place, that is, some inches below the extreme point of our main-yard, and at about half a foot distance asunder. Their appearance lasted some minutes, and made a great impression on the crew, who did not understand its cause. I must confess, that in the utter darkness, amidst the howling of the storm and the roaring of the water, there was something awful in the sight.

Our passage was rendered tedious by contrary winds. On the 22nd of February, we crossed the meridian of the Isle of France, three hundred and forty miles off the island, in very stormy weather, and heard afterwards at St. Helena, that a hurricane raged at this time near the Isle of France, causing great damage to many vessels, and to some of them the loss of their masts. We should have probably shared in this danger had we been a hundred miles nearer the coast. I must here recommend every navigator, if possible, to keep clear of the two isles of France and Bourbon, from the middle of January till the middle of March, as, during that season, violent hurricanes continually rage there, which are very destructive even on shore.

On the following day we passed the large frigate Bombay, belonging to the English East India Company, having on board, as passengers, the Governor of Batavia, Baron vander Kapellen, and his lady, with whom we afterwards had the pleasure of forming an acquaintance in St. Helena. On the 15th of March we doubled the Cape of Good Hope. It had been my intention to anchor in Table Bay, but a storm from the north-west came just in time to remind us how dangerous the bay is at this season, and we prosecuted our voyage to St. Helena. On the 25th of the same month, having traversed 360 degrees of longitude from east to west, we had lost a day, and were therefore compelled to change our Friday into a Saturday.

On the 29th we anchored at St. Helena, before the little town of St. James, the whole crew being cheerful and healthy; but our spirits were soon damped by the news of the death of the Emperor Alexander, which we now received. I must here not omit to express my most cordial thanks to the Governor of St. Helena, for his very kind reception of myself and companions, and for his constant endeavours to make our stay on the island agreeable; he gave dinners and balls for our entertainment, and was always ready to comply with our wishes; hence he granted us what it is usually difficult to obtain—permission to visit the celebrated estate of Longwood, where Napoleon closed his splendid career, in powerless and desolate loneliness. We rode thither one fine morning, on horseback. The little town of St. James lies in a ravine between two high, steep, barren lava-rocks; its pleasant situation and cheerful aspect presenting a striking contrast with the gloom of its immediate environs. By a serpentine road cut through the rock, we climbed an ascent, by nature inaccessible; this path, in some parts not three fathoms in breadth, is bounded on one side by the perpendicular rock, and on the other overlooks an abrupt precipice, from which however it is defended by a strong stone balustrade, so that however fearful in appearance, its only real danger lies in an accident which sometimes happens, that large fragments detach themselves from the superincumbent rock, and roll down the precipice, carrying before them every thing that might obstruct their passage to the bottom.

Having with some difficulty reached the highest ground on the island, we found the tropical heat changed into a refreshing coolness, and enjoyed an extensive prospect over the island, which presented a totally different aspect from that under which it is viewed by passing vessels. The sailor sees only high, black, jagged, and desolate rocks, rising perpendicularly from the sea, and every where washed by a tremendous surf, prohibiting all attempts to land except at the single point of St. James: his eye vainly seeks round the adamant wall, the relief of one sprig of green; not a trace of vegetation appears, and Nature herself seems to have destined the spot for a gloomy and infrangible prison. From these heights, on the contrary, the picturesque and smiling landscape of the interior forms the most striking contrast to its external sternness, and suggests the idea of a gifted mind, compelled by painful experience to shroud its charms under a forbidding veil of coldness and reserve.

This remark only, however, applies to the western part of the island, which is protected from the trade-wind. The higher eastern part, where Napoleon lived, is as dead and barren as its rocky boundary. The trade-wind to which this district is constantly exposed, brings a perpetual fog, and drives the clouds in congregated heaps to the summits of the mountain, where they frequently burst in sudden and violent showers, often producing inundations, and rendering the air damp and unwholesome for the greater part of the year. The ground is for this reason incapable of cultivation; and a species of gum-tree, the only one to be seen in the neighbourhood of Longwood, by its stunted growth of hardly six feet, and its universal bend in one direction, proves how destructive is the effect of the trade-wind to all vegetable life. The nearer we approached the boundaries of the circle within which alone the renowned prisoner was permitted to move, the less pleasant became the country and the more raw the climate, till about a German mile from the town we found ourselves on the barren spot I have already described. Here a narrow path leads down an abrupt descent into a small valley, or basin, surrounded by hills, sheltered from the wind, and offering in its verdant foliage and cheerful vegetation, a refreshing and agreeable retreat. "There rest the remains of Napoleon," said the guide given us by the governor. We dismounted, and proceeded to the grave on foot. An old invalid who watches it, and lives in a lonely hut in its vicinity, now came towards us, and conducted us to a flat, tasteless grave-stone surrounded by an iron railing, and shaded by fine willows, planted probably by the last dependents of the unfortunate prisoner. It is a melancholy thing to tread this simple grave of him who once shook all Europe with his name, and here at last closed his too eventful life on a lonely rock in a distant ocean. The stone bears no inscription, but all who behold it may imagine one. Posterity alone can pronounce a correct judgment on the man who so powerfully influenced the destinies of nations. Honesty may perhaps have been the only quality wanting to have made him the greatest man of his age.

The invalid filled a common earthen jug with clear delicious water from a neighbouring spring, and handed it to us with the remark, that Napoleon, in his walks hither, was accustomed to refresh himself with cold water from the same vessel. This little valley being the only spot where he could breathe a wholesome air, and enjoy the country, he often visited it, and once expressed a wish that he might be buried there. Little as his wishes were usually attended to, this was fulfilled.

After spending some time in contemplating this remarkable memorial of the vicissitudes of fortune, we inscribed our names in a book kept for the purpose, and again mounting our horses, rode to what had formerly been the abode of the deceased; where, deprived of all power, the deposed Emperor to the last permitted the voluntary companions of his exile to address him by the titles of "Sire," and "Your Majesty." On quitting the garden scenery of the pretty little valley, the country resumed its dreary and sterile character. A ride of about a German mile through this inhospitable region, uncheered either by the fragrance of flowers or the melody of birds, brought us within sight of an inconsiderable level, or table land, perfectly barren, crowning the summit of one of the highest hillocks into which this huge rock is divided. In the centre of the plain, and enveloped in so thick a fog that it was scarcely perceptible, stood a small unpretending mansion. "That," said our guide, "is Longwood, late the residence of Napoleon." We soon reached the house, expecting to find it as left at the death of its illustrious occupant; with how much interest should we not have visited it, if nothing had been changed or removed! But the English authorities had not taken our gratification into their consideration. The house is divided into two distinct portions; the smaller half, or Napoleon's sleeping apartment, has been converted into a stable, and the larger into a warehouse for sheep-skins, fat, and other produce of the island.

We had been informed that Napoleon had laid out a little garden near his dwelling, in which he often worked, assisted by Madame Bertrand; and, after many fruitless attempts, had been at length rewarded by the blossoming of a few hardy flowers, and the successful plantation of some young oaks; that one of the latter was set by the hand of Napoleon himself, another by that of Madame Bertrand.

As we could see nothing resembling a garden, I enquired of our guide where it lay; he pointed, with a sarcastic smile, to a spot which had been routed up by hogs, saying, "Here Napoleon was as successful in rearing flowers as he had once been in founding empires, and both have equally vanished." Some oaks are still standing beside a broken hedge, but whether planted by Napoleon or not, no one can tell. We were also shown a pretty house, which had been built for Napoleon by the King's command, but which was not complete till a very short time before his death. Though much better and more convenient than the one he inhabited, he never could be induced to remove to it; perhaps already conscious of the approach of death, he felt no farther concern for the accommodations of life.

Strongly contrasted with the gloom and sterility of Longwood, is the summer residence of the Governor of St. Helena, lying on Sandy Bay, on the western shore of the island, and about half a German mile from the town. In this beautiful and healthful climate, every tropical plant flourishes in the greatest luxuriance. We were hospitably received at Plantation-house, a handsome, spacious, and convenient building, surrounded by an extensive park. In this delightful spot nature and art have combined at once to charm and to surprise; yet while breathing its pure and fragrant air, would our thoughts unconsciously revert with sympathy to the melancholy fate of the exile of Longwood.

The environs of Sandy Bay would be a perfect little Switzerland, but that the glaciers are wanting to complete the resemblance. Scattered amongst the enormous masses of rock which lie confusedly heaped upon each other, a frightful wilderness and most smilingly picturesque landscape alternately present their contrasted images to the eye. Such are the traits which the hand of Nature has impressed upon the scenery in this fortunate portion of the island; while that of man, busily engaged in adding to her charms, and in correcting her ruggedness, throws an appearance of life, comfort, and civilization over the picture. Convenient roads wind up the steep ascents, and frequent openings in the cliff, present vistas of fruitful fields, tastefully built mansions surrounded by parks and plantations, and snug farm-houses embosomed in their pretty gardens. Every thing bespeaks industry and comfort. The inhabitants are all well-dressed, healthy, and contented.

Of their hospitality we had the most agreeable evidences. Invited with friendly cordiality into their houses, we were entertained with the best they had, and with the kindest expressions of pleasure in welcoming the first Russians who had ever visited their country.

We were invited to dinner by one of the richest land proprietors of the island, who, although considerably more than seventy years old, still retained the animation and vigour of youth. This intelligent and well-educated man had never, till his sixty-ninth year, left his beautiful home, except for an occasional and short visit to the town. Through the medium of books, and conversation with the strangers visiting St. Helena, he was well versed in the customs and localities of Europe, and felt the highest respect for the perfection to which the arts and sciences of civilized life had been carried in that quarter of the world, but without experiencing any desire to see it; suddenly, however, at this advanced period of his life, curiosity got the better of his love of ease; his wish to become personally and more accurately acquainted with the much-praised institutions, and the wonderful capital of England, was no longer to be repressed, and he determined to undertake the voyage. On landing in London, he was, as he expressed himself, astonished and dazzled by the extent and magnificence of the city. The throng in the streets, which he compared to ant-hills, far exceeded the ideas he had formed; he visited the manufactories, and observed with wonder the perfection of their machinery; the theatres enchanted him, and the succession of new sights and impressions produced an effect resembling a perpetual intoxication. After a time, however, he experienced the fatigue incident to an extreme tension of mind, and began to sigh for the calm retirement of Sandy Bay, to which he took the first opportunity of returning, never to leave it more.

We passed nine very agreeable days at St. Helena, and shall always retain the liveliest remembrance of the kindness shown us by its amiable inhabitants. My crew, though healthy, had in some degree suffered from the effects of a nearly three years' voyage, and I was anxious during our stay here to strengthen them by a regimen of fresh provisions, (which, however, are very dear upon the island,) particularly as we had again to cross the line, and that in a region often considered unhealthy.

On the 7th of April we sailed from St. Helena, and cut the equator on the 16th in the longitude 22° 37'. Here, delayed by calms, and oppressed by the heat and damps, notwithstanding all my precautions, a nervous fever broke out among the men; and, after having escaped so many dangers, we began to apprehend a melancholy conclusion to our voyage.

This misfortune had probably been communicated to us by contagion. The homeward-bound ships of the English East India Company, which almost all touch at St. Helena, having nothing in view but a quick passage, and the profit resulting from it, do not generally, as I have myself had opportunities of observing, pay that proper attention to cleanliness and wholesome diet which is absolutely necessary to health. During our residence at St. Helena, several of these ships were lying in the roads with sick on board. It is true that, according to a standing order, no vessel is allowed anchorage there till a surgeon has examined into the state of health of her crew; but the captains find means to evade the investigation, and thus are the healthy liable to become infected by association with the diseased.

Half our crew lay sick, and our skilful and active surgeon was unfortunately of the number. A favouring gale, however, sprang up, which carried us into a cooler and drier climate, our invalids quickly recovered, and we escaped with the loss of one sailor only. By the 12th of March, when we passed the Azore Islands, the crew was again in perfect health. On the 3rd of June we reached Portsmouth, where we stopped some days. On the 29th we touched at Copenhagen, and on the 10th of July joyfully dropped our anchor in the roads of Cronstadt, from whence we had sailed nearly three years before.

If my readers have by this time become sufficiently acquainted with me to interest themselves in my affairs, they will not learn with indifference, that my most gracious Sovereign the Emperor has honoured me by the most condescending testimonials of his satisfaction, and that after our long separation, I had the gratification of finding my wife and children well and happy.

REVIEW OF
THE ZOOLOGICAL COLLECTION
OF FR. ESCHSCHOLTZ,
PROFESSOR AT THE UNIVERSITY OF
DORPAT

IT may easily be conceived, that in a sea-voyage a naturalist has fewer opportunities of enriching his collection, than when travelling by land; particularly if the vessel is obliged to pass hastily from one place to another, with a view to her arriving at her destination within a limited period. During our three years' voyage, little more than the third of our time was spent on shore. It is true, that curious animals are occasionally found in the open sea, and that a day may be pleasantly passed in examining them; but it is also true, that certain parts of the ocean appear, near the surface, to be almost wholly untenanted; and accordingly a passage of eleven weeks produced only ten species of animals: these, however, being met with only at sea, are still but partially known to the naturalist, and were the more interesting to me, as, during the preceding voyage, I had become acquainted with many remarkable productions of the ocean. My best plan will be, to arrange in a chronological order all the zoological observations which offered in the course of this voyage. The first, then, was the result of a contrary wind, by which we were detained much longer than we intended in the Baltic, and thus enabled to use our deep fishing-nets upon the great banks: these brought to light a considerable number of marine animals. Upon the branches of the *spongia dichotoma*, some of which were twelve inches in length, sat swarms of *Ophiura fragilis*, *Asterias rubens*, *Inachus araneus*, *I. Phalangium*, *I. Scorpio*, *Galathea strigosa*, and *Caprella scolopendroides Lam.* We obtained, at the same time, large pieces of *Labularia digitata*, *Sertularia abietina*, upon which nothing of the animal kind was to be seen, but attached to which was frequently found *Flustra dentata*; also *Pagurus Bernhardus*, *Fusus antiquus*, *Rostellaria pes pelecani*, *Cardium echinatum*, *Ascidia Prunum*, *Balanus sulcatus*, *Echinus saxatilis*, and *Spatangus flavescens*. Two different species of *Actiniæ*, seated on stones, were brought up, which were not to be found either in *Pennant's British Zoology*, or in the *Fauna danica*.

During a calm, by which we were detained two days on the Portuguese coast, *Janthina fragilis* and *exigua*, *Rhizophysa filiformis*, and another species, were brought up. Many specimens of the *Janthina exigua* were found, the bladder-like mass of which was stretched out to a great length, and bent into the form of a hook at the end. On the outer side was observed a fleshy streak, bordered by a close row of small paunches: these paunches, which were externally open, contained a great quantity of brown atoms, apparently spawn, and evidently in motion. With respect to the *Rhizophysæ*, it has been discovered that they are of the same genus as the *Physsophora*, the hard part being torn away in the act of catching them; upon this occasion also, several of these separated parts, still in motion, and bearing some resemblance to salpas, were brought up, and accurately examined.

Off the Cape de Verd Islands, in addition to the *Exocœtus volitans*, which abounds there, various specimens of the much larger *Exocœtus exsiliens* of Cuvier alighted on board our vessel. The latter species is distinguished by the long black fins of the belly, and by its remarkably large eyes, differing greatly from the species described by Gmelin under the same denomination.

The calms near the Equator afford an abundant harvest to the zoologist, the tranquil water presenting an immense variety of marine animals to his view, and allowing him to take them with little trouble in a net. The open woollen stuff used for flags offers the most convenient material for making these nets, as it allows the water to run through very quickly, and does not stick together. A short, wide bag should be made of this stuff, which may be stretched upon the hoop of a cask, and the whole fastened to a long, light pole. From the height on which we stand above the water, it is impossible to perceive the smaller animals; the best way therefore to catch these is, to hold the net half in the water, as if to skim off the bubbles of foam from the surface; then, after a few minutes, if the net is drawn out, and the interior rinsed in a glass of fresh sea-water, one may frequently have the pleasure of seeing little animals of strange forms swimming in the glass. In the course of ten days, I obtained, in this way, thirty-one different species of animals, among which was a small *Diodon*, eight small crustacea of forms almost wholly unknown; a sea-bug (*Halobates micans*); three species of Pteropodes, closely allied to the *Cliodora*; a small and remarkable Hyalœa; two new *Janthinæ*, *Firola hyalina*, *Pyrosoma atlanticum*, *Salpa cœrulescens*, and another unknown; *Porpita glandifera*, and a new species of globular form; a *Velella*; two new species of Acalephes, of the same family as the *Diphyes*; and further *Pelagia panopyra*, and two other very small species. When the sea was a little agitated on the Brazilian coast, we frequently saw the large sea-bladder floating on the surface; here we also caught with our net a new species of small *Hyalœa*, and of the fin-footed *Steira*, which approaches the nearest to the *Limacina*.

Brazil has lately been visited by eminent naturalists, who have spent years in the country, and have travelled through it in every direction; we are therefore bound to suppress the few detached observations we were able to make during the short space of four weeks.

Captain Von Kotzebue having frequently sent his people to fish in the Bay of Boto Fogo, we enriched our collection by thirty-two kinds of fish, the greater part of which were very similar to those already described as tenants of the Atlantic, but still differing from them in some respects.

How abundant the insects of Brazil are is generally known, particularly in the warm and moist lands along the coast, in the vicinity of Rio Janeiro. Few of them crawl on the ground; the greater part of them live on the leaves and fruits, or under the bark of trees, in flowers, and in the spongy excrescences of the trees. Among the coleoptera, the *Stachylinus* is a rarity: the white-winged *Cicindela nivea* of Kirby is to be found in great abundance on the sand of the beach, which is of the same colour as itself; the *Cic. nodicornis* and *angusticollis Dej.* on the other hand, frequent the paths in the forests. *Cosnania*, which supplies the place of our *Elaphrus*, is found among the grass by the side of brooks. The little animals of the *Plochionus* and *Coptodera* species climb, by means of their indented claws, along the moss on the trunks of the trees: their numbers, in these extensive forests, must be immense. Of the *Cantharis*, the number is small; the strongest of which is the *Cantharis flavipes* F. the descriptions of which vary, so that it may still be doubted whether we have a correct account of it. To show the proportion of the numerous subdivisions which we observed in the different genera, it will be sufficient to give the numbers of those which we were able to collect during the short period of our stay:—these were, *Elater*, 37; *Lampyris*, 17; *Ateuchus*, 14 (including the *Deltachilum* and *Eurysternus*); *Passalus*, 13; *Anoplognathidæ*, 14; *Helops*, (including *Stenochia* and *Statira*) 17; *Curculionidæ*, 108; *Cerambycidæ*, 101; *Cassida*, 24; *Haltica*, 26; *Doryphora*, 12; *Colaspis*, 15; and *Erotylus*, 12. The *Phanæus*, according to MacLeay, distinguished by the total absence of claws from the feet, is peculiar to the warmer parts of America: *Onthophagus* is not met with along the shore, but is found in the interior. Such large *Copris* as are seen in the old world, (*Isidis, Hamadrias, Bucephalus,*) have not been discovered here: their place is supplied by the large *Phanæi, Faunus, bellicosus, lancifer,* &c. A golden-green *Copris* is a great rarity. *Onitis* seems to be quite wanting in America: all the specimens, in this part of the world, that have been placed in that class, belong partly to the *Phanæus*, and partly to the *Eurysternus* Dalm. a remarkable species of the genus Ateuchus.

The *Ateuchi* are not less numerous in South America than in Africa; and here is found what may be looked upon as the intermediate link between *Copris* and *Onitis*. No part of the world is so rich in *Rutelides* as tropical America; and according to the narrow limits within which Mac Leay confines this family, it would seem to be exclusively restricted to this continent. The greater part have not the head divided from the head-shield by a line, and the breast is lengthened in front into a spine: this extensive division is peculiar to America. In the second division, the head-shield of which is bounded by a strongly marked line, those which are provided with a breast-bone are American. South America possesses also the intermediate genus between the *Rutelides* and *Scarabæi*, in the genus *Cyclocephala*, *Anoplognathidæ* were hitherto known to us from New Holland, Asia, South Africa, and South America, and are characterised by the drooping form of the upper-lip, falling lowest in the middle, and by the inequality of their claws; the under-lip, at the same time, has either a projection in the centre, or consists of two parts lapping over one another. In the same way that the *Anoplognathidæ* of New Holland have the appearance of *Rutelides* proper, are the South American *Anoplognathidæ* distinguished by their resemblance to *Melolonthidæ*: those of Brazil have no breast-bone, and at least one claw to each foot is cloven, which distinguishes them from those of Asia. *Chelonarium* and *Atractocerus* fly about in the evening, and are attracted by a light. The Brazilian jumping beetles differ, almost all of them, in their form, from those of Europe. Among the *Heteromerides*, in the neighbourhood of Rio Janeiro, owing to the dampness of the soil, no unwinged beetle is to be met with; a few varieties of the species *Scotinus* have been found upon the Organ mountains only.

Owing to the excessive roughness of the weather, our passage from Rio Janeiro to the Bay of Conception afforded us but few opportunities to add to our collections. A snipe blown out to sea from the Rio de la Plata, a specimen of *Diomedea Albatros* at Terra del Fuego, a large *Salpa*, and a *Lepas*, were all we were able to obtain. The Bay of Conception presents a rich field to the ornithologist. A kind of parrot, with a long tail, and naked round the eyes, flies about in swarms; and a smaller kind from the interior, is to be found tame in the houses; our guns frequently brought down two small kinds of doves. Of *Ambulatores* we met some, of the genera *Cassicus*, *Motacilla*, *Muscicapa*, *Pyrgita*, *Saxicola*, *Cotile*; of birds of prey, *Percnopterus Jota Mol.*, and two buzzards; of *Grallatores*, two kinds of *Hæmatopus*, both with white legs, the one with a black body, as *H. niger* is described by Quoy and Gaimard, the other more similar to the European; a *Vanellus* with spurs to the wings, *Numenius*, *Scolopax*, *Phalaropus*, *Ardea Nycticorax*; and lastly a small bird with remarkably short legs, digitated, and with a short thick bill, frequenting the sea-shore, and feeding on seeds of *Rumex* and *Polygonum*, and constituting a new species, which may be called *Thinocorus*. Of aquatic birds, there were two kinds of *Sterna* and *Larus*; many thousands of *Rynchops nigra*, which were so numerous as to appear like clouds when they rose into the air; a *Procellaria* of the variety *Nectris*; two kinds of *Podiceps*, and an *Aptenodytes* of the variety *Spheniscus*. The upper part of the latter was of a lead colour, and the lower part white, with a line of dullish grey running from the bill to the belly, and forming a boundary between the two colours; the bill and legs quite black. The animal was alive when brought to us.

When resting, it lay upon its belly and stretched out its head. In the water it appeared unable to maintain itself afloat except by incessant paddling, the whole of the body being meanwhile under water.

Of amphibia, only five kinds can be distinctly named; a brown *Coluber*, two small lizards of the family of *Scincoidea*, a small *Rana*, with a spot like an eye on the belly, and a small *Bufo*. Of fishes, the most remarkable was a *Torpedo*, with the back of a reddish brown, and smooth; and a *Callorhynchus antarcticus*: the latter may very well remain in the class of *Chimæra*. Of crustaceæ, we collected three *Canceres*, a *Portunus*, a *Porcellana*, a *Sphæroma*, and a *Ligia*.

The dry land along the coast is extremely poor in insects. The number of beetles collected in 1816, together with those taken on the present occasion, amounted only to sixty seven, but they are altogether peculiar to the country. The most remarkable are a *Carabus* of the beautiful colours of the *hispanus*, but with narrow striped cases to the wings, and a large *Prionus*: the joints of the feet, in this latter, are short and cylindrical, constituting a distinction from the whole family of the *Cerambycinæ*; in every other respect it is unquestionably a *Prionus*, and may be called *Pr. Mercurius*, on account of two wing-shaped appendages, attached to the neck-corselet. Sixteen Carabicides were found belonging to the *Calosoma*, *Pæcilus*, *Harpalus*, *Trechus*, *Dromius*, and *Peryphus*. We were surprised at finding so few dung-beetles. We met with only two large ones, namely, the *Megathopa villosa* of *Esch.* Entomography, forming a species of the *Ateuchus*, and a *Copris torulosa*, described in the same work; this, however, is owing to the very little moisture in the atmosphere, which dries the dung almost immediately. It is curious, that all the seventeen kinds of *Copris* of South America known to us, have but seven stripes upon each wing-case; whereas those of the Old World have eight: the larger kinds, *Hamadrias*, *Bucephalus*, and *Isidis*,[4] alone agree with the South American in the number of stripes. Of the Americans, the *C. Hesperus Oliv.* is the only one with a border to the seventh stripe, and the *C. Actæon Klug* of Mexico is the only one that has eight stripes.

Various kinds of beetles in Chili seek a shelter from the rays of the sun in the dry cow-dung: almost all the Heteromerides with wings grown together, the greater part of the beetles armed with trunks, and several Carabides, were found there. The ten kinds of Heteromerides, with distorted wings, found here, belong to five new classes: the other Heteromerides consist of a *Helops* and a black *Lytta* with red thighs. Of beetles furnished with a proboscis, we met with four kinds of *Listroderes*, two remarkable *Cryptorhynchi*, and a few others of the shape of a *Rhigus*. Lastly are to be noticed, a *Lucanus* of the form of the *femoratus*, a large *Stenopterus*, and a large black *Psoa*. We found very few other species of insects, but several kinds of *Pompilus*, one two inches long, and a curious *Castnia*, were the most remarkable.

Of marine animals there remain to be noticed—a small *Octopus*, a *Loligo*, two *Chiton*, *Patella*, *Crepidula*, *Pilcopsis*, *Fissurella*, *Calyptræa*; of *Concholepas*, only empty shells; a large *Mytilus*, a small *Modiola*, *Turritella*, *Turbo*, *Balanus*; and a Holothuria of the variety *Psolus*.

In the vast sea between the coast of Chili and the Low Islands or the dangerous Archipelago, very few animals appear to live near the surface, at least we saw none; a quantity of flying-fish were seen, resembling the *Exocœtus volitans*, but having the rays of the breast-fins parted towards the end. During the short space of ten days that we stayed at O Tahaiti, the inhabitants, who for a trifling remuneration brought us all sorts of marine animals, enabled us to make acquaintance with all the natural productions of this much praised country. Birds are scarce in the lowlands along the coast. The little blue *Psittacus Taitianus* frequents the top of the cocoa-palm; the *Ardea sacra* walks along the coral reefs; but it is seldom that a tropical bird is seen on the wing. A *Gecko* of the species *Hemidactylus* lives about old houses; a small lizard of the family of *Scincoidea*, with a copper-coloured body and a blue tail, and a striped *Ablepharus*, are met with frequently among the rocks. Of fishes, the variety is great, many of them of splendid colours, particularly the small ones, which feed upon the coral, and seek shelter among its branches. The same place of refuge is chosen by numbers of variegated crabs, more particularly the *Grapsus*, *Portunus*, and *Galathea*. Three kinds of *Canceres* already known were brought us, the *maculatus*, *corallinus*, and *floridus*; the two former move but little, and their shells are as hard as stones. A small *Gelasimus* burrows under the ground, and makes himself a subterranean passage from the water to the dry land. The female has very small claws, but the male has always one very large pink claw, which is sometimes the right and sometimes the left.

A large brownish *Gecarcinus* lives entirely on the land, in holes of his own making; his gills accordingly are not open combs, but consist of rows of bags closely pressed together, and somewhat resembling bladders. *Hippa adactyla* F. is very frequent here, and keeps itself concealed under the sands on the sea-shore. It was from these that Fabricius, who has given a wrong description of their legs, formed his species *Hippa*; Latreille mentions them by the name of *Remipes testudinarius*. Six kinds of *Pagurus*. Of Crustacea already described, *Palæmon longimanus*, *Alphœus marmoratus*, and *Squilla chiragra*; the legs of the last are red, and formed like a club; it uses them as weapons of offence or defence, and inflicts wounds in striking them out by a mechanism peculiar to itself. The number of insects collected on the low land was very small; among them the *Staphylinus erytrocephalus*, also a native of New Holland; an *Aphodius*, scarcely to be distinguished from the *limbatus*

Wiedem. of the Cape of Good Hope; an *Elater* of the species *Monocrepis*; of *Oedemera*, three varieties of the species *Dytilus*, to which belong the *Dryops livida* and *lineata* F.; two small varieties of *Apate*; *Anthribus, Cossonnus, Lamia, Sphinx pungens*, and a large *Phasma*.

No place could be more convenient for the observation of the Mollusca and Radiata than Cape Venus. At a few hundred paces from the shore is a coral reef, which at low water is completely dry. In the shoal water, between the reef and the shore, is found the greatest variety of the more brittle kinds of coral, and among their sometimes thick bushes, mollusca and echinodermes lie concealed. The rapid movements of a small *Strombus*, which, when taken, beat about it with its shell, formed like a thin plate of horn, and armed with sharp teeth, were very curious. On breaking the stone which is formed by fragments of coral, a *Sternaspis* was found burrowing in the interior. Seven classes of Holothuria were examined; three belonged to the species of *Holothuria*, called by Lamarck *Fistularia*, but which name had already been given by Linnæus to the tobacco-pipe fish; the fourth was a species newly discovered, and to which we appropriated the name of *Odontopyga*, because the fundament is armed with five calcareous teeth; the belly is furnished with small tubes, and the back covered with bumps. Two more belong to the species *Thyone*; and the seventh kind of Holothuria ought, properly speaking, to form a class apart, not having tubular feet, but adhering, by means of their sharp skin, to extraneous objects, on which account they might be called *Sinapta*; their feelers are fringed and they live concealed among stones. We found five small kinds of sea-leeches; and among three kinds of star-fish, the *Asterias Echinites*, the large radii of which easily inflict a severe wound; another had the form of the *Asterias Luna*, was eight inches in diameter, without radii, and had more the appearance of a round loaf of bread somewhat flattened. Of corals, the variety was very great, as may be judged from the circumstance of our having collected twenty-four kinds within so short a space of time. *Fungia* is quite at home here; for, independently of *F. agariciformis, scutaria*, and *limacina*, a long kind was also found, having, like the two former, only one central cavity; they are found in shallow water among other corals. Of tabular corals already known, there remain to be mentioned, *Pavonia boletiformis, Madrepora prolifera abrotanoides, corymbosa, plantaginea*, and *pocillifera*.

The inhabitants of the Navigator Isles brought us the little *Psittacus australis, Columba australis*, and another very prettily marked dove, having green plumage, ornamented with a dark violet line across the breast, and the feet and head of a reddish purple. It climbed about the sides and roof of its cage, did not leave its perch when it wanted to drink, but stooped down so low as merely to hang by its legs; it would not eat seed, but lived principally on fruit, particularly bananas, all which closely agreed with the habits of parrots.

During our passage to the equator, *Sterna solida* and *Dysporus Sula* alighted frequently on our vessel, and allowed themselves to be taken. The latter, when old, has a blue beak and red feet; when young, a red bill and flesh-coloured legs. The exterior nostrils are entirely wanting; but in every part are air-cells between the skin and the muscles.

Besides these animals, six varieties of *Pteropodes* were caught; also a *Glaucus*, differing from that of the Atlantic *Janthina penicephala* Per., a *Planaria*, *Salpa vivipara* Per., a *Pyrosoma*, resembling that of the Atlantic, and a *Lepas*, attached to the shell of the *Janthina*. Our collection of Acalephi was extremely rich; of fourteen kinds taken, only one, *Physalia Lamartinieri*, was known to us.

Our eight days' stay at the coral island Otdia, afforded us an opportunity to observe or collect about one hundred different kinds of marine animals. It has already been mentioned elsewhere, that the only kind of mammalia found upon this island is a middling-sized cat, which feeds on the fruit of the pandanus tree, and makes its nest in the dead branches, which it easily hollows out. Several lizards have also been found in these islands, such as the striped *Ablepharus* of O Tahaiti, and a small *Gecko*; a large coal-black lizard was several times seen, but always escaped among the dry pandanus leaves. The fishes are remarkable for the singularity of their form, and the beauty of their colours; those brought to us by the inhabitants belonged to the *Holocentrus*, *Scarus*, *Mullus*, *Chætodon*, *Heniochus*, *Amphacanthus*, *Theutis*, and *Fistularia*.

Of Crustacea we saw twenty different kinds; among them a *Gonoplax* of the middling size, and as white as the coral-sand, among which it lives, on the shore. The *Hippopus* found here differs from the *maculatus* already known by the much greater elevation of its shell. The large *Tridachna* is the *Tr. squamosa Lam*. It is very unusual to meet with an animal belonging to the family of Lepades in tubular holes made in the coral rocks, as is the case with the *Lithonaetta N*. Among the twenty kinds of tabular coral here observed, there was not one of those collected at O Tahaiti; there were three new *Distichoporæ*, *Seriatipora*, six kinds of *Madrepora*, two *Porites*, four *Astrea*, *Pocillopora cærulea*, and another kind, forming broad, yellow, leafy masses, the slime of which stings like a nettle; *Cariophyllæa glabrescens Cham.*, and *Tubipora*, with red animalculæ.

A calm of several days, between eighteen and twenty degrees of north latitude, during our passage to Kamtschatka, afforded opportunities for the observation of several remarkable animals. A small animal of Lamarck's family of Heteropodes, with two rows of separate fins, received the name

Tomopteris. Secondly, a *Salpa*, of the class which lives apart and has fine long fibres projecting from the hinder part of the body. Thirdly, a small animal, nearly allied to the *Diphyes*, the soft part of the body, which contains the tube for receiving nourishment, having no air-bladder. Fourthly, a small *Beroe*, having the power of drawing in its fins. Fifthly, a very small *Porpita*. The sixth animal was a very remarkable crab, the triangular shell on the back, only two lines in length, provided with a spike from eight to ten lines long, (*Lonchophorus anceps,*) projecting both before and behind. Professor Germar has given to a species of beetle the name *Lonchophorus*, but the same had already been described by Mac Leay, under the name of *Phanæus.* Seventhly, an animal belonging to the class *Arthrodiæ,* (*Arthronema N.*) the exterior consisting of stiff tubes, in the interior of which is afterwards found a skin, which eventually divides into separate parts. Eighthly, a *Clio*, about a line in length, with a projection from the globular part of the body. Ninthly, a second variety of *Appendicularia*, described by my friend and companion, on board the Rurik, A. von Chamisso, in the tenth volume of the *N. Acta Acad. Leop. Car.*, which proved to be a species of Mollusca belonging to the Heteropodes of Lamarck. Tenthly, a *Pelagia*, scarcely, if at all, to be distinguished from the *Panopyra Per.* Lastly, a new kind of *Cestum*, *C. Najadis N.*

In the thirty-fourth degree of latitude, renewed calms again enabled us to add to our collection, firstly, a new species of Physsophorides (*Agalma N.*); secondly, a new *Diphyes*; thirdly, a new *Pelagia*, with a yellow skin on the belly, attached to which was a small Cirrhipede of the class *Cineras*; fourthly, a Medusa, with broad belly-bags, and four strong fins; fifthly, a Medusa of the same species, with five and six fins; sixthly, a very small Entomostracea of a flat form, and distinguished by its blue glossy colour, similar to that of the *Hoplia farinosa*; seventhly, a *Loligo*, probably *cardioptera Per.*, remarkable on account of the largeness of its eyes; eighthly, a second species of *Phyllirhoe*, placed by Lamarck among the Heteropodes, to which class it does not, however, belong. The species found in the South Sea has no eyes, and plain feelers; on which account it was formerly considered by us as forming a distinct class, and called *Eurydice.* But, although the *Phyllirhoe* is found to vary so remarkably in its formation, owing to the want of feet, still I consider it as nearly allied to the *Eolidia.* Ninthly, a new *Glaucus*, of a remarkably slim body, with short fins, and of a blackish-blue colour. Tenthly, a *Eucharis N.* In addition to these, no less than eight Crustacea were taken in the net. In the vicinity of Kamtschatka, the vessel sailed daily through red masses floating on the surface; on drawing up some of the water, the pail was found full of red *Calanus*, a line and a half long, with rough feelers of the same length as the body.

In Kamtschatka we found the Bay of Awatscha poor in Mollusca and radiated animals, owing probably to the inconsiderable ebb and flood. The objects most frequently met with, were an ugly little *Turbo*, the empty shell of which was tenanted by a black *Pagurus* and a *Balanus*. A large *Cyanea* differs from the European *C. ciliata*, in the form of the stomach. Another Medusa, constituting a new kind of *Sthenonia N.*, was observed; its digestive organs resemble those of the Aurelia; and about the edge, eight bunches of very long fibres project, provided, like those of the Physaliæ, with two rows of suckers.

The environs of St. Peter and St. Paul, lying under fifty-three degrees of north latitude, possess an insect Fauna, such as is in Europe only found in sixty and seventy degrees of latitude; as for instance, in Lapland and Finland. A great number of species are exactly similar in both regions; others of the Kamtschatkan insects have been met with nowhere else, except in Siberia, and a small number is quite peculiar to the former country. All have not yet been subjected to a diligent examination, and only the following can be with certainty mentioned.

Firstly, in the North of Europe also, are found: *Pteroloma Forstroemii Gyllh.*, *Nebria arctica Dej.* (*hyperborea Schoenh.*), *Blethisa multipunctata*, *Pelophila borealis*, *Elaphrus lapponicus* and *riparius*, *Notiophilus aquaticus*, *Loricera pilicornis*, *Poecilus lepidus*, *Dyticus circumcinctus*, *Staphylinus maxillosus*, *Buprestis appendiculata*, *Elater holosericeus*, *Ptilinus pectinicornis*, *Necrophorus mortuorum*; *Silpha thoracica*, *lapponica*, *opaca*, and *atrata*; *Strongylus colon*, *Byrrhus albo-punctatus*, *dorsalis*, *varius* and *aeneus*; *Hydrophilus scarabæoides* and *melanocephalus*; *Cercyon aquaticum*, *Hister carbonarius*, *Psammodius sabuleti*, *Trichus fasciatus*, *Oedemera virescens*, *Apoderus Coryli*, *Leptura trifasciata*, *atra* and *sanguinosa*, *Lema brunnea*, *Cassida rubiginosa*, *Chrysomela staphylæa*, *lapponica*, *ænea*, *viminalis*, *armoracea* and *vitellinæ*; *Eumolpus obscurus*, *Cryptocephalus variegatus*, *Coccinella* 7 *punctata*, 13 *punctata*, *mutabilis*, and 16 *guttata*. Secondly, such as have been hitherto found only in Siberia, though their number is but small: *Cantharis annulata Fisch.*, *Dermestes domesticus Gebl.*, *Aphodius ursinus N.*, and *A. maurus Gebl.*, and *Leptura sibirica*.

Among the beetles which have as yet been met with nowhere else, and are therefore considered peculiar to the country, may be named: a *Cicindela*, between *hybrida* and *maritima*; a *Carabus* of the form of the *cancellatus Illig.*, with black feelers and legs; *C. Clerkii N.*, and another, green, with gold border, of the form of the *catenulatus*, caught near the line of perpetual snow on the volcano Awatscha: *C. Hoffmanni N.*, *Nebria nitidula*, which is the same as the *Carabus nitidulus Fabr.*, as appears by that preserved in Banks's Museum, hitherto the only specimen in Europe; great numbers of these are found in the valleys: a second black sort was caught on the volcano. Further, a small bright yellow *Pteroloma*, an *Elaphrus*, *Bembidia* six kinds,

Agonum four kinds, an *Omaseus*, an *Amara*, *Elater scabricollis Esch. Entomogr.*; an *Elater*, like *undulatus* P., three kinds, which like *Bructeri*, live among stones; a wingless kind which is found buried in the sea-sand, and a perfectly black *Campylus*.

Besides these, a beetle forming a peculiar species between *Atopa* and *Cyphon*; *Cantharis cembricola Esch.*, and one resembling the *testacea*; a *Hylecoetus*, scarcely differing from *dermestoides*; *Catops*; a *Heterocerus*, broad and covered with whitish scales; an *Elophorus*; two *Phaleriæ* with a black ground; two kinds of *Stenotrachelis*, both larger than the European, which has hitherto borne the name of *Dryops ænea*; and in fact, the beetle in Banks's Museum, so called by Fabricius, is either the same, or a species very nearly resembling it, and it may therefore be conjectured that some mistake has accidentally occurred in the designation of its native country in that Museum. There still remain to be mentioned a Chrysomela, like the *pyritosa*, and a *Coccinella* with five very large spots upon both wing-covers, found on the line of perpetual snow on the volcano. It is also probable that the valley of the Kamtschatka river, although lying farther north than the environs of the Awatscha, yet possesses a richer in sect Fauna, as the climate there is much milder, and adapted to agriculture.

From Kamtschatka our course lay mostly eastward. At first the sea was strongly luminous every night; but when in the midst of this immense ocean, it one night happened, that while the ship was as usual surrounded by brilliant waves, a dark precipice seemed to open before it. On reaching this part of the water, it appeared that all the luminous matters, such as Zoophytes and Mollusca with their spawn, were entirely wanting, and from this point to the American coast the sea remained dark.

We remarked generally of this great ocean, that on the Asiatic coast, even at a considerable distance from land, (as much as thirty degrees west from Japan,) the water is always muddy; it is made so, partly by the great numbers of small Crustacea, Zoophytes, and Mollusca, partly by the impurities of the whales and dolphins, which latter especially, as well as many other kinds of fish, are very numerous here from the abundance of food to be found. On the contrary, the sea in the neighbourhood of the north-west coast of America is clear and transparent, and nothing is found in it except here and there a single Medusa.

In the principal settlement of the Russian-American Trading Company on the island of Sitcha, in Norfolk Sound, we had better opportunities of becoming acquainted with natural productions than elsewhere, as, during our stay there, in the year 1825, from March to the middle of August, we had an almost uninterrupted continuation of fine weather: we were in this respect peculiarly favoured, as in most years this island does not enjoy above one fine day to fourteen cloudy or wet ones. We ourselves experienced this sort of weather in 1824, when we passed the latter part of August and the beginning of September there.

Of the Fauna of this island, about two hundred and sixty species came under our notice: from its immediate vicinity to the continent, it is not wonderful that several large *mammalia* are to be found. Among these is the *Ursus Americanus*, of the black race; a fox; a stag, which perhaps does not differ from the *Cervus virginianus*, and the common beaver, which feeds on the large leaves of a *Pothos*, said by the inhabitants to be injurious to man. Besides these are observed a small *Vespertilio* with short ears, a *Mustela*, and a *Phoca*.

Of birds we remarked: the *Aquila leucocephala, Astur, Corvus Corone* and *Stelleri*, and some varieties of the species *Turdus, Sylvia, Troglodytes, Parus, Alcedo, Picus, Ardea, Hæmatopus, Scolopax, Charadrius, Anas*, and *Colymbus. Trochilus rufus* is not only often found here, but also under sixty degrees of latitude. A small shoal of *Procellaria furcata* was once driven into the Bay by stormy weather. Of Amphibia, only a small kind of toad is met with. There is no great variety in the kinds of fish, but the individuals are numerous, especially a well-flavoured sort of salmon, and herrings; a *Pleuronectes* several feet long, and a reddish yellow *Perca* two feet long and very thick, are extremely abundant.

The number of accurately examined *Annulides* amounts to sixteen, among which are found some of very fine and unknown forms. Most of them belong to the well-known species *Cirrhatulus, Arenicola, Aceronereis, Nereis, Aphrodita, Serpula, Amphitrite*. A *Nereis* was found swimming on the surface of the water in the middle of the bay, which measured two feet in length, and one inch in thickness; the appendages at its sides resemble round leaves. An *Aphrodita* several inches long, and very narrow, was not rare. An animal resembling the Amphitrite kind is found enveloped in a transparent mass like jelly.

Of Mollusca we observed, a *Limacina*; two *Eolidiæ*, some of which have very beautiful colours; a *Laniogerus*; a *Polycera*; four kinds of *Doris*; a *Scyllæa*; an animal which deserves the name of *Planaria*, it was three inches long, two broad, and only half a line thick; on the upper surface, half an inch from the edge, are two projecting eyes; and in the same part, on the surface beneath, the mouth may be perceived; in the middle of this under surface is another aperture, from which the animal, when in a tranquil state, frequently stretches out four small folds of skin; this creature, like the *Planariæ*, crawls very nimbly. Besides these, a small *Onichidium*, and a new kind of shelled snail.

In the mossy woods live a large, yellowish, black-spotted *Limax*, and two Helices of middling size. In the bay itself are found a few of the gilled snails with spiral shells; and a considerable number on the outward coast, which is washed by the ocean. Here are several species of the genera *Murex*, *Fusus*, *Buccinum*, *Mitra*, *Trochus*, and *Turbo*. Further, there are found here a large *Fissurella*, and six species of a genus which, from its simple, unwound shell, would be immediately taken for a *Patella*; the creature, however, closely resembles the *Fissurella*, with the difference that only one gill is visible in the fissure over the neck. It is remarkable, that on the whole north-west coast of America down to California, no *Patella*, only animals of the genus *Acmæa*, were to be met with. Of the *Chiton* genus, six species were observed; in one, the side skin covers the edges of the shell so far as to leave only a narrow strip of it visible down the back; in others, the shell is entirely concealed under the external skin. It is worthy of remark, that these latter, as well as one similarly formed, found in California, attain the considerable length of eight inches. A third kind, to be reckoned among this subdivision, Pallas obtained from the Kurile Islands, and has described it as *Chiton amiculatus*.

Among the Acephala are to be named a large *Cardium*, also found on the Californian coast; *Modiolus*, two species; *Mytilus*; *Mya*, two species; and *Teredo palmulatus*: the latter, which is brought here by the ships, is very mischievous in the harbour, and attains to the length of two feet. In this species are comprehended three *Ascidiæ*, of different forms; one *Anomia*, one *Terebratula* attached to a *Fusus*, two *Lepas*, and a *Balanus*. Six *Holothuria*, belonging to three different species, were observed: a large *Thalassema* gave us a long-wished for opportunity of observing, that this species belongs to the Holothuria, and not to the Annulides. Eight species of star-fish are found here, partly on the rocks, and partly at the bottom of the sea: among them, four are furnished with five *radii*, and the rest with six, ten, eleven, and eighteen: the latter sort, which is the largest, lives at the bottom of the sea, and the number of its *radii* varies from eighteen to twenty-one. Only one *Ophiura* was seen. Several kinds of very large *Actinia* inhabit the rocks: all that we examined belonged to the species which is externally provided with rows of teats. A *Velella* also was caught in the open bay: this is the first which has been observed in so high a latitude.

Of *Zoophytes*, some presented themselves of the genera *Antipathes*, *Millepora*; *Cellaria*, *Flustra* two species, *Melobesia*, *Retepora*, *Acamarchis*, *Lafœa*, *Aglaophenia*, *Dynamena* fives species, *Clytia* four species, and *Folliculina*, two species. The *Antipathes* consists of a simple stem resembling wood, which grows to the length of ten feet: it grows at a great depth in the open bay, and is often accidentally drawn up in fishing.

Although of all insects of this island the beetle is the most numerous, yet during the whole spring and summer, in almost daily excursions, with constant fine weather, only one hundred and six kinds were found. On the whole, it may be observed, that none among them belong to any of the species which have been hitherto considered as peculiar to America; yet there are some of them which form entirely distinct classes, and must therefore be natives of the north-west coast of America. The result of close examination was, that none of those found here are to be met with either in the north of Asia or in Europe, and only seven species are to be found even in Unalashka.

The Fauna is adapted to the climate and the soil; *Nebria, Patrobus* and other Carabides, find a cool abode among the stones on the banks of the ice-cold brooks which fall from the snowy summits of the mountains; in the fir-woods, live several kinds of *Xylophagi* and some *Cerambycides*; the old mossy trunks of fallen trees afford hiding-places for several kinds of Carabides, as two *Cychrus, Leistus, Platysma*; and for *Nitidula, Scaphidium, Agyrtes*, and *Boros*. On the skirts of the woods, shrubs and tall plants nourish some insects belonging to various families; as two *Homalisus, Omalium*, and *Anthophagus, Anaspis, Cantharis*, and *Silis*; besides *Elater* of eight kinds, and a ninth living under stones.

The small standing waters, formed by single cavities, are proportionably rich in water-beetles, among which is found a *Dyticus* of the form of the *sulcatus*, seven *Colymbetes, Hydroporus* two species, and a *Gyrinus*. The Carabides are: *Cychrus angusticollis* and *marginatus, Nebria metallica* and three new species, *Leistus, Poecilus* two, *Patrobus, Omaseus adstrictus, Platysma* two, *Loricera* plainly distinguished from the *pilicornis, Amara, Trechus* three, *Bembidium* two, and *Leja* three species. Thirteen species of *Brachelytra* have been found; of carrion-beetles, a *Necrophorus*, a *Silpha*, quite of the figure of the *subterranea*, and a *Catops*. Of Pentamerides are still to be mentioned the *Scydmaenus, Cryptophagus, Byrrhus, Cercyon, Psammodius*, and *Aphodius*. The number of Heteromerides amounts only to four; namely, one *Boros* of the arched form of the *elongatus*, a small *Phaleria*, a pale yellow *Anaspis*, and a small black, flat beetle with overgrown wing-cases of a new form, which must be reckoned among the family of the Blapides. Of beetles with probosces only six were found, of Xylophagi seven, of the species *Hylurgus* two, *Bostrichus* three, one *Rhyzophagus*, and a larger quite red *Cucujus*. The three stag-beetles were a *Sphondylis*, a *Lamia* with excrescences upon the sharply pointed cases of its wings, and a beetle of the flat form of a *Callidium*. Of the large class of Chrysomelides, only five varieties were to be met with; namely, two sorts of *Donacia*, a beetle of the form of a *Lema*, and two varieties, of the form of Eumolpes. Lastly, three Trimerides were discovered, namely, two *Latridii* and a *Pselaphus*.

Our stay in the Bay of St. Francisco, in California, during the months of October and November, was unfavourable to the observations of a naturalist. A perfect drought prevails during those months; vegetation appears completely dead; and all birds of passage abandon the country. The landscape along the coast is alternately formed of naked hills, of a rocky or clayey soil, and low sandy levels, covered with stunted bushes. Further inland, the soil is more fertile, but still deficient in wood. The background every where presents lofty mountains; we visited only those to the north, at the foot of which the Russian settlement Ross is situated. Here a fine forest of lofty pines, mingled with oak and horse chesnut-trees, charms the eye. Of the mammalia of this hitherto unexplored country, only a few can be cited. The light grey American bear, with a small head, abounds in unfrequented districts, but brown bears are also occasionally killed. We nearly ascertained the existence of two sorts of polecats, and succeeded in getting a skin of one; its fur is brown below, and black above: from the forehead a white stripe runs to the middle of the back, and then divides into two, which extend to the extremity of the tail. The feet of the animal show that it treads upon its entire sole, and lives in holes like a badger. The second sort is said to have three white stripes: our sailors caught one, but it got away again. The mole here is larger than in Europe; the upper part of the body is of a greyish brown, the lower part an ash grey; the legs are covered with a white fur, and the taper tail is one-fifth of the length of the body. A shrew-mouse also was caught. Two or three kinds of large cats are said to have been seen; a *mustela*, something of the nature of the *Lutreola*, was shot near the Rio Sacramento. The sea-otter still abounds here, but its hair is brownish, and not black. The *Cervus Wapiti* is found in great numbers in hilly districts; and there are deer in all unfrequented places. The back and sides of the latter are of a reddish brown in summer, in winter of a blackish brown; the belly, breast, and inside of the legs are white; the mouth, forehead, and the exterior of the ears are black. The antlers (of the male) divide into a fork, with round smooth branches. The animal grows to the height of two feet and a half. Near the Rio Sacramento, and in the vicinity of the Russian settlement, we saw herds of animals of the shape of goats, with long hair hanging from their legs, and short straight horns; we were unfortunately unable to obtain a specimen; we saw the animal only through a telescope, and judged it to be the *Capra Columbiana*, or *Rupicapra Americana Blainville*, so often spoken of. Lastly, we have to mention a small kind of hare, not so large as a rabbit, found in great abundance among the bushes, and a dormouse seen in the southern plains.

In consequence of the lateness of the season, most of the birds that breed here had already left the neighbourhood; we therefore saw only such birds as pass the winter here, and also a number of aquatic birds that were daily arriving from the north. Of the former we met with five kinds of *Icterus*; one quite black, except the shoulders, which were red; these were extremely numerous, and sleep, like the *Icterus phœnicius*, among rushes. The *Sturnus ludovicianus* and *Picus auratus* of the United States, are also found in California; the *Percnopterus californicus*, *Corvus mexicanus*, and *Perdix californica*, are already known. A large grey crane, probably from the north, remained here: upon the whole, the number of birds observed, amounted to forty.

A few Amphibia were found concealed under stones; namely, a large *Tachydromus*, a *Tropydurus*, a *Crotalus*, a *Coluber*, and four *Salamandrides*: among the latter was one with the body covered with warts, and a narrow compressed tail, the glands of the ear wholly wanting; the others had long narrow bodies of about the thickness of a common earth-worm, with short legs, standing far apart, and toes scarcely perceptible to the naked eye.

Nearly two hundred kinds of beetles were collected: with the exception of the *Lampyris corrusca Fabr.*, which, according to Banks, is found on the Columbia river, all are as yet undescribed. Upon the dry ground, under stones, many Heteromerides, with distorted wing-cases, were found, and among them six new species. A large *Cychrus* was also found, and a species closely resembling the *Manticora*, together with many other Carabides, of which we collected, in all, fifty different species.

It was at the Sandwich Isles that the greatest number of fishes and Crustacea were collected: of the former the greatest variety, and the most remarkable, were kept in the fish preserves of the royal family. Of other classes of animals, but few are to be met with. Among the dense woods that cover the backs of the mountains, there must be a number of land-birds, but we met only *Melithreptus vestiarius*, and two sorts of the *Dicæum*; in the fields laid under water were the *Gallinula chloropus* and a *Fulica*. Of corals there is but little variety; these islands being situated nearly in the highest latitude in which coral is ever found. In the vicinity of the harbour are two sorts of *Astræa*, two *Porites*, a *Pavonia*, and a *Hornera*. The number of insects is small, as is indeed the case with all land animals; it is therefore creditable to our industry, that we are able to muster twenty sorts of beetles. A small *Platynus* is the only Carabide; in the water, two *Colymbetes* and a *Hydrophilus* were found. The only *Elater* belongs to a species (*Agrypnus N.*) in which we reckon various specimens found only in the Old World, such as *Elater tomentosus, fuscipes, senegalensis*, &c.; beetles which have two deep furrows in the lower part of the neck-shield, to receive the feelers, and which go in search of their food at night. They resemble many of the European springing beetles covered with scales, and included by Megerle under the name Lepidotus; such are *fasciatus, murinus, varius*. Two Aphodii were found; one, of the size of the *Psammodius porcatus*, but very flat, lives under the bark of a decayed tree, the wood of which has become soft. Another has the almost prickly shoulders of the *Aphodius stercorator* and *asper*, of these we form the species *Stenocnemis*, and include therein four new varieties found in Brazil and Luçon. It may be here observed, that *Psammodius sabuleti* and *cylindricus* N., must be classed with *Ægialia*, which, on account of the horny nature of their jaws, and the projection of the upper lip, enter into the same class with *Trox*; the remaining kinds of *Psammodius*, however, do not at all agree with the character given them by Gyllenhal, and ought in their turn to be classed with *Aphodius*. Among the remaining beetles, all of which dwell under the bark of trees, a *Parandra* was the largest.

During our two months' stay in the Bay of Manilla, we could only become acquainted with a small part of the natural productions, in which the large island of Luçon appears extremely rich, because it is difficult to procure them without travelling far into the interior; but the country round Manilla and Cavite being cultivated to the distance of several days' journey, the woods of the mountains alone remain in a state of nature. There dwell the gigantic snakes and crocodiles, of which every one has some tale to relate. A small *Cercopithecus* is found in great abundance; but we were not able to meet with a good drawing, or even a tolerable description of it. Skins of *Galeopithecus* were brought us; and we were assured that the animal allowed itself to be tamed, and would sit like a monkey, and take its food with the fore-feet. Two kinds of flying dogs, one of them apparently a *Pteropus edulis*, were shot and eaten in the neighbourhood. Two other animals, of the bat kind, belonged to the classes *Hypexodon* and *Nycticejus*. A *Chelone*, three feet long, was brought us, remarkable for seven shields on the middle of its back. *Terrapene tricarinata* is abundant. We obtained also a *Basilicus*, a large *Tupinambis*, and two *Geckos*, which do not as yet appear to have been described. *Achrochordus fasciatus* lives in the sea, and is frequently brought up in the nets of the fishermen; on land, it is unable to move from the spot on which it is placed.

In November and December, the months we passed at Manilla, all the insects had concealed themselves; and it was only by the assistance of several active Malays, who were all day long hunting them, that we were able to collect upwards of two hundred beetles. Upon the whole, the beetle Fauna agrees with that of Java, of which island many have already been made known. A *Tricondyla* we had ourselves the pleasure of catching on the trunk of a tree: the inhabitants did not bring them to us, as they suppose them to be large ants, and are apprehensive of being stung by them. We obtained three sorts of *Catascopus*, nineteen aquatic *Scarabæus*, six *Hydrophilus*, five *Buprestis*, five *Melolontha*, four *Anomala*. *Scarabæus Gideon* is found in great abundance in the thick bushes, where it climbs up the branches by means of its long legs and large claws. Of *Oryctes nasicornis*, a Malay one day brought us no less than sixty, taken out of some decayed wood. A green *Cetonia*, of the size and form of the *chinensis*, of a coppery brightness, is rare. Three small Lucanides, of those called by Mac Leay *Nigidius* and *Figulus*, are found in the wood of living trees.

Of wingless Heteromerides, we found only one *Tagenia*, and that under the dry bark of a tree. For Pimeliades the soil is unfavourable, there not being, as far as we could learn, in the country round Manilla, either stones, or low, broad-leafed plants, under which these animals can find shelter from the burning rays of the sun: they are found only under dry bark, and about the root of the *Opatrum*, *Uloma*, and similar plants. The Helopides, on the other hand, must be looked for on the dry branches in the tops of trees, but we obtained only six varieties. Of the twenty-six stag-beetles collected here, it is necessary to observe, that they are all essentially different from those found in South America.

Our passage through the Chinese Sea was rapid; and as we had constantly stormy weather in the Indian Ocean, we had no opportunities of observing marine animals. In the vicinity of the Cape, we caught some Salpæ, Physaliæ, and Velellæ; but in the Northern Atlantic, after reaching the region of the *Sargassum natans*, daily opportunities for interesting observations presented themselves. From the point at which the floating sea-weed was first noticed, (eighteen degrees north latitude, and about thirty degrees of longitude west of Greenwich,) to the coast of England, forty-three kinds of animals were observed, not noticed on our outward voyage. We were able to make a very exact examination of the whole system of the *Beroe punctata*. Three new varieties of Medusa were discovered, and an animal (*Rataria N.*) between *Velella* and *Porpita*: it has the flat form of the latter, but is provided with a sail, which it can draw in at will. We also caught the animal which Le Sueur has called *Stephanomia uvæformis*. Lastly, we had the good fortune to procure a specimen of an animal which appears to form a link between the *Salpa* and *Pyrosoma*. This species (called *Anchinia*) consists of a number of animalculæ of the Salpa form, which, by means of a stalk, are attached to a common body, all of them being turned to the same side.

In the course of less than three years, 2400 kinds of animals were either examined, or only collected, consisting of the following classes:—

	Species.
Mammalia	28
Birds	165
Amphibia	33
Fishes	90
Annulides	40
Crustacea	127
Insects	1400
Arachnides	28
Cephalopodes	20
Gasteropodes	162
Acephali	45
Tunicati	28
Cirrhipedes	21
Echinodermates	60
Acalephi	63
Zoophytes	90

FR. ESCHSCHOLTZ.

Dorpat, 7th January, 1828.

THE END.

FOOTNOTES

[1] A kind of urn in use throughout all Russia, called a Samowar, or self-boiler. It generally stands in the middle of the tea-table, and is furnished with a large kettle for water, and a space filled with fire to keep it boiling.

[2] The baidars, or canoes of the Aleutians, are generally twelve feet long and twenty inches deep, the same breadth in the middle, and pointed at each end. The smaller are suited only for one man, the larger for two or three. The skeleton and the keel are made of very thin deal planks, fastened together with the sinews of the whale, and covered with the skin of the sea-horse cleared of the hair. It has a kind of deck made of this skin, but leaving an aperture for each person the canoe is intended to carry. These sit in the bottom with their legs stretched out, and their bodies rising through the apertures, which are but just large enough to allow them to move and row conveniently. The space between their bodies and the deck being so well fitted with bladders, that no drop of water can enter.

These baidars are moved very rapidly by oars, and the Aleutians put to sea with them in all weathers.

[3] This applies only to the lower classes; the Yeris are nearly all as large as at Tahaiti.

[4] This kind was known to Fabricius, for *Copris Midas* is a variety of the male, and *Gigas* is the female. The former has erroneously been deemed a native of America.

Lightning Source UK Ltd.
Milton Keynes UK
UKHW010745271222
414464UK00004B/309